Praise for
8 Minute Meditation

"The meditation book everyone has been waiting for. This is a brilliant book that makes meditation accessible to anyone who has the slightest interest in the subject. Eight minutes a day will change your life forever."

—Richard Carlson,

author of *Don't Sweat the Small Stuff . . . and it's All Small Stuff*

"The perfect program for busy people who want a real spiritual practice. *8 Minute Meditation* introduces you to meditation quickly and with integrity. If you think meditation would be good for you but aren't sure where to start—*buy this book!*"

—Susan Piver,

author of *The Hard Questions:*
100 Essential Questions to Ask Before You Say "I Do"
and producer of *Joyful Mind: A Practical Guide to Buddhist Meditation*

"As a strong believer in the value of meditation, I welcome this new book. It should enable even the busiest of us to experience the many benefits of this ancient technique. Mr. Davich guides us with wit, sensitivity, and charm. Importantly, he is a realist, mapping the many opportunities to apply meditation during our daily lives, and expertly teaching us how."

—Barrie R. Cassileth, Ph.D.,

Laurance S. Rockefeller Chair in Integrative Medicine,
Memorial Sloan-Kettering Cancer Center

continued . . .

"How long does it take to experience inner peace and tranquility? This clear and simple book can help you find the time to calm and clear your mind through meditation no matter how busy you may be. I heartily recommend it."

—Lama Surya Das,
author of *Awakening the Buddha Within*

"Here's a Deep Spiritual Truth about this little book: It delivers on its promise! Victor Davich distills profoundly important information about how to meditate into an extremely user-friendly package and delivers it fresh and crystal clear. Who knew eight minutes could get so real?"

—Jeffrey M. Schwartz, M.D.,
author of *The Mind & The Brain* and *Dear Patrick*

"If you feel drawn to meditation but haven't been able to start, *8 Minute Meditation* opens the gate to the garden. Victor Davich invites us down the path of lovingkindness and awareness, with step-by-step guidance and good humored encouragement."

—Tara Brach, author of *Radical Acceptance:*
Embracing Your Life with the Heart of a Buddha

"An extraordinary and definitive ecumenical approach to this sacred yet often confusing discipline. *8 Minute Meditation* will enhance, deepen, and enrich the spiritual practice of anyone, regardless of their faith tradition."

—Reverend John Newton,
The Christian Institute, Santa Monica, CA.

1
2
3
4
5
6
7

VICTOR DAVICH

8 Minute Meditation

QUIET YOUR MIND. CHANGE YOUR LIFE.

A PERIGEE BOOK

Neither the publisher nor the author is engaged in rendering professional advice
or services to the individual reader. The ideas, procedures, and suggestions contained in this book are not intended as a substitute for consulting with your physi-
cian. Meditation should only be done in a safe, comfortable environment, and
should not be done while operating a vehicle, device or equipment of any nature.
Neither the author nor the publisher shall be liable or responsible for any loss or
damage allegedly arising from any information or suggestion in this book.

A Perigee Book
Published by The Berkley Publishing Group
A division of Penguin Group (USA) Inc.
375 Hudson Street
New York, New York 10014

Perigee trade paperback edition: July 2004

Visit our website at www.penguin.com

Library of Congress Cataloging-in-Publication Data

Davich, Victor N., 1952–
8 minute meditation : quiet your mind, change your life / Victor Davich.
p. cm.
ISBN 0-399-52995-0
1. Meditation. I. Title: Eight minute meditation. II. Title.

BL627.D375 2004
158.1'2—dc22   2003069643

Printed in the United States of America

10 9 8 7 6 5 4 3 2

CONTENTS

PREFACE

IF YOU ARE reading these words, there's something drawing you to meditation.

Maybe you've heard that meditation can help you become more peaceful and feel safer in a complex, uncertain, and often harsh world. Perhaps there's another reason. Maybe you don't even know why.

But you do know you'd like to learn to meditate. Only problem is, meditation sounds really complicated and extremely time-consuming. If only you could find a simple way to meditate that would suit your lifestyle yet provide the benefits you long for . . .

Well, here's good news: You've found it! And all it takes is 8 minutes a day.

8 Minute Meditation is the revolutionary new program that will change your life as easily as it fits into it. In just 8 minutes a day—the space between two television commercials—you can build a lifetime meditation practice. *Time* magazine calls it "the most American form of meditation yet."

8 Minute Meditation

BEGINNINGS

IF YOU HAVE ever thought, *I'd love to meditate, but it's too hard and takes too long,* it might be because the meditation books and programs you've come across are overly complicated, confusing, and time-demanding.

Until now.

8 Minute Meditation is a modern approach to meditation, bringing you Eastern tools for Western results. Whether you have never tried meditation before or tried it and stopped, *8 Minute Meditation* will work for you. It's designed for who you are and the way you live today.

Not only does the 8 Minute Meditation program work, it does something most other meditation books don't: It makes meditation practice enjoyable, pleasant—even fun—to learn. Not only will this meditation program turn you into a real meditator, but you'll enjoy smiles, chuckles, and maybe a few outright belly laughs along the way. This is entirely in keeping with the spirit of meditation. It's also the best way to help you learn to meditate.

And don't worry, I never sacrifice substance for laughs. I've got more than twenty-five years of meditation experience and have already written a Book of the Month Club selection on the subject. As such, I am a grateful example of how the practice of meditation can transform your life. Every word in this book is intended to help you do the same.

So, please, join me on a journey that will quiet your mind, change your life—and just plain make you happier. I'll be with you every step of the way. And you'll be glad you came along.

We live in an age in which we have less free time than ever. Any activity we undertake, from refinishing a floor to learning meditation, must be:

- Simple to understand

- Easy to do

- Offer benefits worth the time investment

It's no wonder that when it comes to meditation, we have little time (or patience) for confusing and complicated explanations of meditation or inscrutable instructions such as "Just do nothing." And we certainly don't have up to an hour a day to meditate.

8 Minute Meditation changes all this. Meditation may be a 3,000-year-old tradition, but *8 Minute Meditation* is a completely new and current approach to it—an 8-week program that's simple, easy, clear, and incredibly time-effective.

With *8 Minute Meditation,* you'll be meditating quickly and easily, starting from Day One. At the same time, you'll be building a steady meditation habit that can last you a lifetime. All this in *just 8 minutes—the space between two TV commercial breaks.*

What's more, you will begin to address—and resolve—the main issues and challenges that brought you to meditation in the first place, such as:

"I feel really stressed out."

"My thoughts are out of control."

"I feel as if I'm drifting through life."

"I keep flying off the handle at my co-workers and family."

"I need some peace in my life!"

"I can't concentrate."

"Something's missing, but I don't know what."

"Everything seems OK, but still, I wish . . ."

8 Minute Meditation is simple, easy meditation for everyone, regardless of age, schooling, or income—even if you think you can't sit still for one minute, much less eight. Whether you're a new parent, a single mom, a high school student prepping for the SAT, or a young executive about to start your dream job, rest assured—*8 Minute Meditation* will work for you. In a matter of minutes from right now, you'll be able to begin your first meditation period. No confusion. No wasted time. No kidding.

Here's how easy it's going to be for you to become a meditator:

1. You'll begin with a short "tour" of meditation that will give you the essentials without confusing or boring you. You'll learn what the word *meditation* means and see how easy it is to meditate. You'll be briefed on how this once-daily 8 Minute Meditation program works—and why it works.

2. Next, you'll prepare and set up for your first meditation period. You'll learn a simple, effective meditation posture that requires nothing more than sitting on an ordinary chair. You'll also receive a unique set of Meditation Operating Instructions that will assist you throughout the next 8 weeks—and hopefully beyond.

3. Then, you'll begin your first meditation period, guided by simple, jargon-free, failure-proof meditation instructions. You'll meditate for just 8 minutes a day—no more and no less. Part II of this book contains 8 sections—one for each week of the program. You'll spend a week with each technique and then move on. Each section also includes material that will help you transition from one week to the next, as well as in-depth answers to frequently asked questions.

4. After you complete your 8 week meditation program, you'll have the opportunity to "upgrade" and deepen your meditation practice. Part III contains everything you'll need to

do this, including a "training schedule" and a special Meditation in Action Template that will enable you to bring meditation into every aspect of your daily life. Part III concludes with a cream-of-the-crop selection of meditation books, tapes, and retreat centers.

With 8 Minute Meditation, getting the hang of meditation is simpler—much simpler—than you think. Of course, you might find the first few days, maybe even the first weeks, somewhat challenging. But hang in there with me. After two weeks, you will be meditating with familiarity. By the end of Week 8, you will be a full-fledged meditator—ready to go even deeper into meditation practice. But what is much more important, you'll reap benefits of meditation from the very beginning. Benefits such as:

- A greater sense of peace and well-being

- Simple, drug-free stress reduction

- Improved concentration and focus

Quite simply, meditation can change your life. I'm not talking about going to Permanent Blissland. What I am talking about is much, much better—the real deal: a way to live in this complex world with clarity, well-being, calm, and happiness.

With all these great things going for it, it's a wonder everyone on the planet *isn't* meditating. So why aren't you? For the answer—and solution—read on.

WHY YOU CAN'T START TO MEDITATE.
WHY YOU STARTED AND STOPPED.
WHY 8 MINUTE MEDITATION CHANGES THAT.

Whenever people learn that I'm a meditator or have written a meditation book, they invariably feel compelled to tell me one of two things: "I would love to learn to meditate. But I just can't," or "I tried to meditate but stopped."

My response to these statements is always and exactly the same: "What do you think is in the way?" Here are some of their responses. Do any strike you as familiar?

WHY I CAN'T LEARN TO MEDITATE

It's too complicated.

It takes too much time.

I'm not smart enough.

I'm too old.

I'm too young.

I'm not patient.

I'm not spiritual.

I'm not special enough.

I don't have the time.

WHY I STARTED MEDITATION AND STOPPED

I couldn't stop thinking.

It took too long.

I went on vacation and couldn't start when I returned.

It wasn't what I expected.

I didn't get enlightened.

I wasn't spiritual enough.

I wasn't special enough.

I must have bad karma.

Although these lists look long, the truth is that all these rationales for not meditating come down to two basic misbeliefs:

- Meditation is obscure, confusing, and hard.
- Meditation takes too much time to learn and actually do.

Let's see how the 8 Minute Meditation program addresses—and eradicates—both these issues.

Meditation Is Too Nebulous, Confusing, and Hard

With more than 4,500+ meditation books on the market, it's easy to see why meditation has an undeserved reputation for being a mysterious, arcane system reserved for a brilliant select few.

But the truth is exactly *the opposite:* Anyone can easily learn to practice meditation, no matter what those convoluted books filled with Sanskrit say. This is the primary goal of *8 Minute Meditation:* to demystify meditation and make it effortless for you to both learn and do.

The 8 week program is divided into three sections:

• Part I provides you with the foundations of meditation and prepares you to immediately start your first meditation period.

• Part II is the heart of the matter: the specially designed, step-by-step, 8-minute-a-day, 8-week meditation program.

• Part III is the "upgrade" section, offering you ways to make your meditation practice deeper and apply it to everyday life.

Sound simple? Sure it does. Because it is.

Meditation Takes Too Much Time—to Learn and Practice

Be honest when you answer this question:

Is your life so super-busy that you don't have 8 minutes a day, when you get up, or just before bed, that you can call your own?

Sure, everyone's life is jam-packed and hectic. But to say that you don't have 8 minutes a day to do something you want to do sounds a tad flimsy, doesn't it? Do you have time to watch 8 minutes of TV, up to the first commercial break of *The Simpsons?* Well, okay, then. You've got time to meditate the 8 Minute Meditation way.

But, you say, I'm a single mom. I'm a traveling dad. I just had a baby! I'm busy, busy, busy. How in the world can I find time to meditate? ! The answer is: The time is there. Just relax and allow yourself to see where it is.

Single mom? How about meditating after the kids go to sleep? Or before they wake up? Traveling dad? Next time you're on that two-hour flight to San Antonio, close your golf magazine and spend 8 pleasant minutes in airborne meditation. New parent? Give baby her 5 A.M. feeding, then meditate for 8 minutes while she dozes off.

And by the way, if you think those short, 8 minute periods won't amount to anything, think again: No lesser light than Albert Einstein said that the most amazing phenomenon in the universe is compound interest. Each 8 minute meditation period is a deposit into your account at The First National Bank of Meditation, where it earns a hefty interest rate. In time, those small deposits aggregate and compound into a huge payoff: the ability to live life in peace and calm.

Where else can you get a greater return on so small an investment?

THE BIRTH OF THIS BOOK: WHY 8 MINUTES. AND WHY IT WORKS.

Now, you're probably asking two things at this point:

- "Why 8 minutes?"

- "Who are you, anyway, to tell me this will work?"

That's the spirit! Like the Great American Bumper Sticker says, "Question Authority." So allow me to introduce myself without, as authors love to do, recounting my personal and fascinating (to the author) spiritual journey.

I tell you my story because I want you to see that my life is similar to yours. People like us don't sit on mountaintops, but have challenging stress-filled lives that demand we get down in the trenches of real life, every day. And if you can take meditation along for the ride, it makes a huge difference.

First off, I'd like you to know that I am the author of *The Best Guide to Meditation,* a very popular guidebook to meditation and a Book of the Month Club selection. I began to practice meditation in 1975, and over those decades, I have meditated for thousands of hours, attended dozens of meditation retreats, and studied with (and count as friends) some of the foremost meditation teachers in America.

I began meditating in New York City while attending law school. My reason for starting was practical, not spiritual: An alumni told me he had started meditating the year before and found that his memory had improved—as well as his grades.

At the time, among other reams of case law, I had to commit a six-inch-thick copy of the IRS Tax Regulations to memory. So I figured, "What have I got to lose?" I attended a couple of nights of basic meditation instruction and was told by the instructor to meditate twice a day.

The first time I meditated, I experienced something I hadn't felt much of in my life, and never, ever in law school. *I felt peace.* And when something feels good, you usually keep on doing it. So I did.

I continued to meditate on a twice-daily basis. After several months, I found myself more relaxed yet, paradoxically, more alert, both in and out of class. I also experienced better concentration and focus. This naturally led to better comprehension of even the most complex materials—such as those inscrutable tax regulations. What was more astounding, I found myself actually looking forward to my daily sparring practice with them.

Then came the final tax exam, and to my (and my professor's) utter surprise, I got an A. Whether meditation had anything to do with it or not, it didn't matter. I knew by then that meditation was something I was going to continue to practice. Which I did, throughout twelve years of legal practice in New York, as a business affairs attorney for two Fortune 500 advertising agencies and Paramount Pictures.

In 1975, I moved to Los Angeles to become more involved in the entertainment business. I became a producer, screenwriter, novelist, and nonfiction writer. In LA, I continued to deepen my meditation practice, moving first to Zen and then on to Vipassana, or Insight Meditation.

During this period, I was fortunate enough to discover several extraordinary meditation teachers who enabled me to go deeper in my practice. They included Sharon Salzberg, Joseph Goldstein, and Shinzen Young, who became my primary teacher and meditation "go-to" guy. The teachings, benefits, and insights I received from these and other teachers were, and remain today, of inestimable value. They're also what I hope to convey to you in this book.

The impetus to write *8 Minute Meditation* came to me after someone told me for the umpteenth time that they'd "really love to meditate, but . . ." Frankly, I was tired of hearing whatever excuse they had come up with. So I set out to create a failure-proof meditation program that would eliminate any and all "buts," and that would:

• Fit into anybody's lifestyle, no matter how busy they were.

• Start people meditating immediately—and make sure they wouldn't stop.

• Provide simple, reliable meditation instruction that anyone could do the first time they tried.

• Anticipate and clearly answer common questions, doubts, and concerns.

• Enable anyone who wanted to go deeper into meditation to be able to do so.

• Be supportive, encouraging, and give people the feeling that I was with them every step of the way.

8 Minute Meditation is the program I created to meet these goals. And, more importantly, help you achieve yours.

Why 8 Minutes?

As far as I know, there is no Geneva Convention governing meditation time periods. Some teachers require students to meditate for up to one hour a day. If you attend a Zen retreat, that can rise to ten hours! On the other end of the spectrum, several meditation books say three or even one minute is sufficient daily meditation time.

Here's why I think 8 minutes a day is just right:

• It's not a long time and will not compromise, intrude on, or throw off your lifestyle. It's the time it takes to take a shower or prepare a tuna salad sandwich. It's also the time between the first two commercial breaks of your favorite sitcom.

• Everyone, and yes that includes you, can fit 8 minutes into his or her day. Can you wake up 8 minutes earlier? Go to bed 8 minutes later? If you're traveling, do you have 8 minutes while waiting for your boarding call or on the plane? After you check in at the hotel? Of course you do.

• A steady, daily, 8 minute practice is cumulative and builds what I call "Mindfulness Muscle." More about this later. For now, just know that it's all good.

BEGIN TO MEDITATE. RIGHT NOW.

Meditation has never been simpler than the 8 Minute Meditation way. You won't find a single word in this book that requires a spiritual or *Webster*'s dictionary, an instruction you can't understand, or a meditation technique you cannot do simply, easily, and the first time you attempt it—like *right now*.

As they say in Hollywood, it's time for a "Preview of Coming Attractions." Over the next 8 weeks, we will be getting into things in a lot more depth. But for right now, I want you to get an idea of how simple and easy it's going to be for you to learn to meditate.

For the moment, don't worry about doing anything but sitting right where you are. All I want you to do is read the following simple instructions and do the best you can.

Remember, this is not a pop quiz. Grades will not be issued. As you'll soon learn, there's no wrong way to meditate.

TASTE MEDITATION

• Sit erect, engaged yet relaxed, as if you're listening to your favorite friend.

• Allow your eyes to close.

• Take a long, deep inhale. Hold it a moment. And just let it go.

• Allow your breath to settle into its own natural flow. Don't force anything.

• Bring your attention to where you feel your breath the most. It could be your diaphragm, chest, or maybe under your nostrils. There's no wrong place.

• Watch your breath from this place for the next five breaths.

• Open your eyes.

CONGRATULATIONS! YOU'RE A MEDITATOR!

Well, you did it! It's easy, right? Not some big deal or something you aren't capable of doing. Actually, meditation is just the opposite: the most natural thing in the world.

So are you ready to do something this pleasant and simple for 8 minutes a day?

Of course you are. Just follow the 8 Minute Meditation program game plan. In 8 weeks, you can have a meditation practice that can last you a lifetime.

I've already said that if you're reading these words, something has attracted you to meditation. You're about to find out what that is.

Just turn the page.

PART ONE

• • •

MEDITATION 101

IN A SHORT amount of time, you're going to begin Week One of your 8 Minute Meditation program. But first, it's important that you get the lay of the land. Just like your home, your meditation practice should rest on as solid a foundation as possible. That's what Part I is about. It's going to:

- Define and demystify what meditation really is

- Tell you what the 8 Minute Meditation program can—and can't—do for you

- Address and resolve some common misconceptions about meditation and resistances to meditation

- Answer beginning meditators' most frequently asked questions

- Provide you with a set of simple, powerful "Operating Instructions" that you will use in the next 8 minutes, 8 weeks—and perhaps for the rest of your life

It may be natural for you to want to skip over this part and "cut to the chase," that is, begin to meditate. But fight off that desire. This stuff is important. You'll have a much better chance at success if you read it with full attention.

WHAT IS MEDITATION?

Meditation is not a static "thing." It's a "doing." This is why it's so hard to put a finger on and define.

Many definitions of meditation are given by the use of metaphors. Here are two examples, one ancient and one modern:

- "It is exactly like muddy water left to stand in a glass. Little by little, the sediment sinks to the bottom and the water becomes pure." (Taisen Deshimaru)

- ". . . like great scuba gear. You can see, hear, touch, and taste your thoughts without drowning in them." (Laurie Fisher Huck)

But these are verbal attempts to describe what is beyond words. Meditation is an active process that is a confluence of the qualities of concentration, insight, and wisdom. Here's how I describe it:

• Meditation is not a noun, but a verb. Meditation is a dynamic *process,* like the liquid flowing state of water as opposed to frozen ice. This is what I mean when I say that meditation is a "doing," what your seventh-grade English teacher called an "active verb."

• Meditation is not the goal; it's the journey. In just the act of sitting down to meditate, you've already achieved your goal. Pretty great, huh? Talk about a win-win situation!

• Meditation is not the menu; it's the meal. Alfred Korzybski, a famous Polish mathematician, once said, "The map is not the territory." The best way to understand the "territory" of meditation is to actually meditate. Otherwise, it's like describing Chunky Monkey Ice Cream to a Martian; you can talk from dawn to dusk, but that poor little alien won't know what you're talking about—until she dips into the Ben & Jerry's container.

Still, I want you to have a definition of meditation you can hang your hat on for the next 8 weeks, something that will keep you from wasting time trying to figure out if you're meditating every time you sit down to meditate—instead of actually meditating.

So let's keep it simple. For the next 8 weeks, the following is declared to be the 8 Minute Meditation definition of meditation:

Meditation is allowing what is.

Right now, please close your eyes, relax, and, for the next minute or so, just feel your body. Your hands in your lap, your feet on the floor. The noise in the street. Now, as alertly as possible, pausing after each word, repeat the definition three times.

Meditation is allowing what is.

Meditation is allowing what is.

Meditation is allowing what is.

Did you get a little taste of meditation? I bet you did. And speaking of meditation, did you know that ...

MEDITATION TASTES GREAT.
AND IT'S GOOD FOR YOU, TOO.

Back in prehistoric times (before MTV), there were those children's television shows where the host would hold up a loaf of bread and proclaim, "Kids, Wonder Bread tastes great! And it's good for you, too!" Well, that's how I feel about meditation.

Why does meditation taste great? The taste of meditation is, quite simply, the taste of peace. And what does peace taste like? Something beyond words—but that you know better than your own name. One of the things your 8 Minute Meditation practice is about is giving you that taste of peace—8 minutes worth—every day.

Why is meditation "good for you," too? It's common sense. When you are in a relaxed and allowing state, you are less mentally agitated. And when you are less mentally agitated, your brain sends fewer stressful messages to your body, allowing it to become more relaxed and healthy.

Medical researchers have, for the past several decades, studied the effects and benefits of meditation. Some of the results indicate that meditation can, alone or in conjunction with other modalities:

- Lower blood pressure

- Reduce acute and chronic pain

- Improve muscle response time

- Relax diaphragm and internal organs

- Increase breathing efficiency and lung capacity

- Reduce anxiety and stress

- Increase recognition of compulsive behavior patterns

The latest research on meditation has been focused in the area called neuroplasticity. Recent research at the University of Wisconsin has shown that a steady practice of meditation over many years can actually encourage the brain to physically rewire itself to be happier (*Time* 8/4/03; *The New York Times Magazine,* 9/14/03)!

But please, before you go rushing off to rewire your caudate nucleus, remember these results relate to brains of people who might have been meditating for at least a few years. Don't be disappointed if, after you finish your first 8 minute period, you don't feel that things have radically changed for you.

Regard this exciting new research as something to shoot for—yet another reason why "Meditation tastes great! And it's good for you, too!"

ROVING MIND: WHAT GETS IN THE WAY OF MEDITATION

This would be a good time to briefly introduce a character you're going to see a lot of in your meditation practice over the next 8 weeks: your Roving Mind. Ironically, it will be your biggest hindrance to meditating—as well as your path to success.

Whether you're a first-time or seasoned meditator, chances are high—about 100%—that when you start to meditate, you will be subject to what appears to be an incessant and absolutely uncontrollable stream of thought. In the Zen meditation tradition, this is called "watching the waterfall"—that perpetual Niagara gushing out of your mind. It's what my pal John Newton calls "cognitive spam."

Invariably, almost all beginning meditators believe that the process of meditation is somehow creating this cascade of thinking. But the fact is otherwise. Your personal Niagara Falls is and always has been there. You've just been too busy *drowning under it* to notice it! Meditation practice affords you, perhaps for the first time in your life, an amazing opportunity: a way to keep warm and dry despite the deluge.

Here's an example of how meditation helps you accomplish this:

Let's say you are halfway into your 8 Minute Meditation period. Your mind is tranquil and peaceful. Suddenly, out of nowhere, the following thought appears: *Gee, my mind seems pretty quiet.* This is the seed of what I call a "thought-story." And here's where it can lead next:

Peace. Yeah! This is what's supposed to happen? ... How can I stay like this? ... Uh-oh, I'm starting to lose it ... Dammit! I've lost it! For God's sake, I can't do anything right ... Like today when I deleted that e-mail from Sarah ... Boy, was Reed mad ... Yeah, well he's a cold fish anyway! ... Speaking of which, they're having a special on poached salmon at the market. Better get some on the way home ...

And on and on and on. Get the picture? You start out in tranquility and peace and wind up shopping for dinner! All in the space of a second. Say hello to Roving Mind.

Now don't start feeling bad that you have a Roving Mind. It's not only you. It's every one of us, 24/7. The mind is a perpetual thought machine whose sole job is to think. It's a loyal, indefatigable worker who will never let you down.

Well then, if you can't stop or suppress your thinking, how do you deal with it so you can live in peace and calm? This is where meditation comes to the rescue with a simple, elegant, and powerful solution: Don't suppress thinking. *Surpass it.*

How in the world can you do this? Well, you can start by remembering your new definition of meditation and "allow what is." And how do you do that? By doing what I call The *Meditation Three-Step:*

1. Recognize that you are thinking.

2. Gently return to meditation.

3. Repeat steps 1 and 2 as needed. (This will be a lot!)

Meditation is the art of gently returning—over and over again. And again. This is why we call it meditation *practice*.

Now, one important note: When I refer to Roving Mind, I'm talking about those pesky, roving, rambling thoughts that continuously drain your energy and just plain drive you crazy. Roving Mind is not the same as and should not be confused with thought *per se*.

You constantly need to do things, get here and there, hold down your job, and pick up your kids after school. It's a blessing that your mind is working all the time, making sure you watch where you're going, avoid trouble, and remember your car keys. There's a difference between a roving "thinking" mind and what we might call "working" mind. As you continue to meditate, you'll be able to distinguish between these different mind-sets with increasing clarity.

We'll get into much more detail about Roving Mind throughout the next 8 weeks. But for now, know that it's not meditation that gives rise to it. You've been doing this your entire life. Isn't it good to finally see it and know that you're about to do something about it?

WHY MEDITATE?

The Roman philosopher Seneca once asked, "What good is a wind without a compass?" This section is going to help you define your personal meditation goal.

Most people come to meditation for myriad reasons, but they usually fall into one or more of these categories:

- Physical health, such as lowering blood pressure

- Mental health, such as lowering stress levels

- Spiritual growth, such as seeking a closer connection to life

Why do you want to learn to meditate? This is a very important question, and you shouldn't feel shy or embarrassed to ask it. There is this misconception that meditation should not be goal-oriented. However, we live in a goal-oriented society. When we do something, we expect—maybe even demand—a result. After all, why put time and effort into something if it doesn't return a concrete benefit? I wouldn't do it, and neither should you.

There is absolutely nothing wrong with having a goal in mind that you'd like meditation to help you achieve. In fact, I think it's a good thing. And to help you define your own meditation goal, take a look at some popular ones:

- You suffer from acute or chronic physical pain. You've heard or read that meditation might help with pain reduction.

- You take medication for stress, anxiety, or hypertension. Your doctor also recommends that you take up meditation.

- You feel anxious and confused. You need a way to "chill out" without resorting to martinis and tranquilizers.

- Life is just dandy. However, you've got "the blahs." You feel something is missing. You don't know quite what that is, but you've heard that some people find their answer in meditation.

• You find yourself angry, irritable, and sometimes acting inappropriately. You've heard meditation can help you get a better handle on your anger.

Now that you've seen some other people's reasons, let's determine *your personal reason* for wanting to meditate. Your response is very important. It will make you aware of the "fuel" that will propel you through these next 8 weeks.

So right now, take a few moments and relax. Close your eyes. See what pops up in your mind to fill in the following blank: "Meditation is a process that can help me _____."

Okay, great! Whatever you came up with was the perfect answer.

You say you want to meditate because you want to be happier? Fine, you want to be happier. Then "Meditation is a process that can help me become happier." You thought about how afraid you were of your own road rage? Okay, your goal is "Meditation is a process that can help me be less angry behind the wheel."

Now you've created the reason to meditate that's meaningful to *you*—not someone else. Copy down this sentence and place it where you can read it before your daily 8 minute meditation period.

Now that you've gotten close and personal with why you want to meditate, let's do the same with the 8 Minute Meditation program and see how simple, yet effective, it can be for you.

HOW THE 8 MINUTE MEDITATION PROGRAM WORKS

The 8 Minute Meditation program is designed to be user-friendly, easy, and effective. Here's all you need to do:

- **Read Part I thoroughly.** Don't skim or skip to Parts II or III.

- **Familiarize yourself with the Meditation Operating Instructions.** These are your "ground rules," designed to keep you on track and maximize your meditation period.

- **Meditate once a day for 8 minutes.** Part II is divided into 8 sections, one for each week of the program. Each week has its own specially selected guided meditation technique. In addition, it contains "check-in" sections on your progress at this point of the program, discussion and tips for this week's meditation technique, a follow up, and a section of frequently asked questions with accompanying answers.

- **Move on after each week.** At the end of each week, simply turn the page and move on to your next meditation week and technique. The techniques have been selected and organized to gradually allow you to deepen your practice. That's why it's good not to skip around—or ahead.

- **Upgrade your practice.** At the end of 8 weeks, you have the option to stay where you are or move on to Part III and deepen your meditation practice. Part III offers several easy and simple ways to do this. It also introduces the Meditation in Action Template, which will show you how you can apply meditation to every single one of your daily activities. I highly and heartily recommend the upgrade. And no matter what, please try the Meditation in Action Template.

WHAT YOUR 8 MINUTE MEDITATION PROGRAM WILL—AND WON'T—DO

The 8 Minute Meditation "Won't" List

The 8 Minute Meditation program won't:

- **Confuse you.** The meditation techniques in *8 Minute Meditation* are so simple a child can do them (and if you've got one, maybe should).

- **Lecture you.** You've chosen this program because you don't want to spend time on the history or philosophy of meditation.

- **Delve into you and your past.** Why go into discussions of mood disorders, brain chemistry, or childhood? As we say in Hollywood, "Let's cut to the chase," meaning, in this case, meditation, right now, in this very moment.

- **Get into religion.** Your 8 minute-a-day meditation program is nondenominational, nonsectarian, and nonpolitical. There are no hidden agendas, Buddhist or otherwise.

- **Enlighten you.** *Enlightenment* is a word indiscriminately bandied about by everyone from New Age gurus to soft-drink promoters. Your 8 Minute Meditation program is about meditation. Don't worry about enlightenment. Just relax and meditate.

• **Ask to be your guru.** Some teachers say that you can't meditate effectively without a guru or master to teach you. I disagree. Everything you need to begin to meditate is right here, in this book.

• **Give you the "secret handshake" or shortcut.** Believe me, if I could, I would. But there are no secrets or shortcuts in meditation. *8 Minute Meditation* is pared down to the essentials. So relax. Meditation doesn't get simpler than this.

• **Leave you in the lurch.** Over the next 8 weeks of this program, I'll be right beside you every step of the way. I've been down this road myself and have anticipated the challenges, questions, and doubts that will come up for you. I've built all kinds of "technical support" into this program. You'll see what I mean when you start Week One.

The 8 Minute Meditation "Will" List

The 8 Minute Meditation program will:

• **Get you meditating right now.** *8 Minute Meditation* is designed to be simple, clear, and user-friendly—to get you up and meditating, *right now*. Look at your watch. In less than twenty minutes from now, you'll be sitting down to your first meditation period.

- **Respect your time and energy.** There never seems to be enough time in the day to do what you have to do—much less meditate. That's why all you're asked for is 8 minutes out of your day. Not ten, twenty, or forty-five. *Just 8 minutes.* Not one second more or less.

- **Give you clear, simple, effective instruction.** The program and this book are 100% jargon-free. You won't find a word you can't understand, a meditation instruction you can't comprehend, or a discussion that loses you in philosophy or technicalities.

- **Enable you to build a real meditation practice in a short time.** Many people have the notion that you've got to *schlep* to Tibet and sit in full lotus posture for months on end to develop a strong meditation practice. Well, that's just not true. If you follow the plan—8 minutes a day for 8 weeks— you will develop a strong, disciplined meditation habit that you can deepen, and can last your lifetime.

- **Answer your basic questions.** Each section of the book contains its own Q&A section. By the way, the answer to every question is always the same. "You're doing great. Follow the program. And keep meditating."

- **Help you over the rough spots.** The unique burning concern, issue, or doubt you have has more than likely been posed by thousands of other meditators. You'll find these questions addressed at many places along the way. Don't feel embarrassed, dumb, or ignorant. We've all been there.

- **Support and encourage you.** I'm with you every step of the way, not only to answer your questions but also to support your efforts. I promise, I truly want to help you get where you want to go.

- **Point you in the right direction.** After you complete your 8 week meditation program, you'll have the opportunity to "upgrade" and deepen your meditation practice. Part III contains everything you'll need to do this, including a "training schedule" and the Meditation in Action Template.

WHAT HAPPENS DURING THOSE 8 MINUTES?

Just about now, you're probably thinking that 8 minutes sounds like a really long time to sit still and do nothing. This is a normal thought and goes to the heart of meditation. So let's clear up two things:

- 8 minutes is not a long time.

- Meditation is not "doing nothing."

I want you to get out a kitchen timer or even your watch and start timing while you read this section.

8 Minutes Is Not a Long Time

You don't have to be Steven Hawkings to know that time is relative. We all know what it means when we say "time just flew." It's an attempt to describe the experience where we are so involved in an activity that we lose track of relative time. The engrossing activity can be as varied as watching an overtime NFL game, participating in a yoga flow class, or just hanging out with a close friend. Whatever it may be, the experience is one of timelessness.

On the other end of the spectrum, we have all experienced time as "an eternity." It's the two minutes you waited at an intersection to make a left turn when you were late to work, the ten minutes in a bank line because the ATM was down, or the twelve minutes listening to an insurance agent describe your medical co-payment. This is time that feels more like an endurance contest than a transient event.

As you can see, time can pass in the "blink of an eye" or last eons. It's all about the attention with which you approach the activity. *8 Minute Meditation* has been created to provide you with a series of meditation techniques that will fully engage your attention. But as Lauren Bacall once said to Humphrey Bogart when she kissed him, "It's a lot better when you help."

So meet me halfway. When you get ready to meditate, don't prejudge what it's going to be like timewise. Don't look at meditation as a horrific burden, boring chore, or—heaven forbid—something that is good for you (a surefire recipe for disaster).

Just set your timer for 8 minutes. And meditate.

Doing Nothing Is Really Something

There is a popular misconception that meditation is "doing nothing." In point of truth, meditation is more "something" than what you think is something!

What do I mean by that? Just this: Whenever you meditate, you are engaged in a process, a "something" that demands your 100% complete focused awareness and attention. In this attention, you are *active,* but in a whole new way: a peaceful, calm way that allows you to cultivate a new relationship with your mind.

This is one of the great benefits of meditation, one you are going to start experiencing once you get your practice underway. But for now, just remember that meditation isn't about "zoning out." It's about "zoning *in.*"

Timing Your Meditation Period

While we're on the subject of time, let's discuss an inexpensive yet extremely important item you must have to meditate properly: a timing device.

Clock-watching during a meditation period is counterproductive. It puts you in a kind of limbo, a state of repeatedly opening your eyes to check on how much time has elapsed and mentally calculating how much time remains. This less-than-optimum situation is easily handled by using a timing device. You set it for 8 minutes and forget it.

To get the most out of 8 Minute Meditation, you need to have a kitchen timer. If you don't already have one, they're available at houseware or electronic stores. This less-than-ten-dollar investment will pay off handsomely in its ability to help you establish the most level playing field possible for meditation. Make sure your timer is an electronic one that does not produce any distracting ticking sound.

Another option is to use the *8 Minute Meditation* Guided

Meditation CD I created for this program. It is a voice-guided version of the meditation instructions contained in this book. The CD allows you to sit down, find the current week's meditation track, push PLAY, close your eyes, and be led through your 8 Minute Meditation. A pleasant gong sound announces when 8 minutes are up. No muss, no fuss. The Guided Meditation CD is available through my website, www.8minutes.org.

Okay, look at your watch or timer. How many minutes did you take to read this? Good. Subtract that from 8 minutes, and you've got an idea of how quickly your 8 Minute Meditation period will pass.

"BUT ISN'T . . . ?" MEDITATION BUBBA MEINTZES.

I've already discussed the two major excuses people have for not meditating: They haven't got time, and it's too hard. Now, we're going to spend a few minutes clearing up some other misconceptions about meditation.

My nanny, Pauline Spector, called them "bubba meintzes." Your grandmother might have called them "old wives' tales." Buddhist grandmas would call them "painting a tiger on your wall." They all mean the same thing: You are creating a problem where none exists. Let's take a look at some of the most popular meditation bubba meintzes:

1. Meditation Is Too Complicated.

Meditation is pretty straightforward. It is not too hard. Nor is it too easy.

Try this, right now:

• Close your eyes. Relax.

• Pay attention to your breath.

• Notice one in-and-out cycle of your breath.

Were you able to completely pay attention to your breath, without thinking, daydreaming, fidgeting, or wondering what the heck you were doing? Most likely not. Amazing, isn't it, how many thoughts you can pack into just one breath, like some infinite, expanding suitcase?

But despite all the mindtalk going on, did you find it so incredibly difficult to watch your breath? Of course not. This is what meditation is: paying attention to something, realizing that you've strayed away from it, and then gently returning to it. Exactly what our *8 Minute Meditation* definition says: allowing what is.

A tourist in Manhattan once stopped and asked world-renowned violinist Yasha Heifetz how to get to Carnegie Hall. His response: "Practice." It's the same with meditation: You just practice and get better at it.

2. Meditation Is a Religion.

There is a popular misconception, especially in the West, that equates meditation with Buddhism. But there's a major difference:

Buddhism, like Judaism and Christianity, is a religion. Meditation is a nonsectarian process of awareness. In fact, you can find a meditative component not just in Buddhism, but in all the great religious traditions, including Christianity and Judaism.

Rest assured, the 8 Minute Meditation program is completely nonsectarian. Its only purpose is to help you develop a meditation practice you can use for your lifetime. There are no other agendas, hidden or otherwise.

3. When You Meditate, It's Like You Are Hypnotized. It Sounds Scary.

It has been shown that brain-wave patterns in meditation states are different from those generated during sleep or hypnosis. This kind of deep relaxation is a naturally occurring phenomenon and should not be cause for alarm. Even in states of deep meditation, you will be as, and even possibly more, aware and alert than in your normal state. This is exactly the opposite of being hypnotized, stupefied or in a trance.

4. Meditation Is an Excuse to Escape from Reality and Responsibilities.

Some people think that meditation is a sneaky, selfish, narcissistic way to avoid responsibilities and real life. Nothing is farther from the truth. The goal of meditation is not to escape *from* life—*but into it*! Here's how that works:

When your mind is calm, focused, and accepting, you experience all aspects of life in a richer, fuller way. This is because you are not judging everything, but allowing it, moment by moment. This new way of seeing can result in the creation of more "life energy" as well as a desire to engage more fully with every aspect of life.

So don't worry. Becoming a meditator doesn't mean you'll wake up and find that you've abandoned your law practice and are heading for a monastery in Bhutan. But it certainly can mean finding more richness in your legal practice, love for your family, and reverence for all forms of life.

5. You Have to Have Absolute Silence to Meditate.

Meditation is about *allowing the world in,* not shutting it out. Most people think meditation can only be done properly in absolute silence, preferably on a mountaintop, far removed from our noisy, crass, everyday world. But that's just not true.

Remember our definition of meditation? "Meditation is allowing what is." Well, this wild, noisy, seemingly uncaring everyday world is, whether you like it or not, "what is." And it includes car alarms blaring, children laughing (and screaming), and your neighbor's stereo blasting hip-hop.

In meditation, we treat all outside intrusions *exactly the same way:* We welcome them, without any judgments or attempts to mute or muffle them by donning actual or "mental" sunglasses, earplugs, or nose clips. You know, we "allow . . . allow . . . allow."

This "allowing" concept was expressed beautifully by Shantideva, an early Buddhist sage, who said, "Where would I possibly find enough leather with which to cover the surface of the earth?

But wearing leather on the soles of my shoes is equivalent to covering the earth with it."

Meditation opens you to an entirely fresh, peaceful, and rewarding relationship with the world, one that embraces everything and rejects nothing. Each time you meditate, you have the opportunity to cultivate a new way to live more peacefully and joyfully—in the midst of that wild and wonderful place known as daily life.

6. If I Meditate, I'll Have to Give Up the Things I Like: Reading *Vogue*, Watching Notre Dame Football, *Seinfeld* Reruns, Burgers, and Starbucks.

Many people think meditation means having to sacrifice the things they love. I call this the "Tofu-Meditation Connection." It comes complete with veggies, soy products, chamomile tea—and zero enjoyment (unless of course you happen to like these things).

You also may have come across teachers and books that say that the requirements to be a meditator include vegetarianism, teetotalling, and perhaps even celibacy. If this were the case, 98% of the meditators I know wouldn't be allowed to meditate! Including yours truly.

The idea that you have to sacrifice things you love is not only erroneous, it's counterintuitive to meditation. Your 8 Minute Meditation program demands no prohibitions on anything—especially so-called "vices." This includes everything from double lattes to watching *Survivor IX* to great sex.

The truth is that once you start meditating, you'll more than likely enjoy these things—and everything else—even more. Why? Because you'll have a richer experience of them. To test this, I want you to try the following *Sweet Mini-Meditation*.

- Find a bite-size morsel of something sweet, such as a raisin or a Hershey's Chocolate Kiss.

- Take the sweet in your hand. Closely examine that beautiful morsel, bursting with sweet potential.

- Very, very slowly, bring the sweet to your mouth and slowly set it on your tongue.

- Close your eyes. *Really get in touch* with the exquisite taste as it begins to dissolve in your mouth over your tongue.

Did you notice how much fuller and richer your experience of taste is when you are fully present in the moment? Imagine doing everything this way.

7. You Can't Learn to Meditate Without the Presence of a Teacher.

Learning any skill is always easier when you have a good teacher. So if you can find one, go for it. However, the reality is that there is a scarcity of good meditation teachers. Finding one is tough enough, and getting to where they are can entail a major investment in time, travel, and money.

This is a major reason why I created *8 Minute Meditation*. The program is one-stop shopping. Everything you need to begin, build, and maintain a real meditation practice is here in your hands. And although I can't be physically in the room with you, I'm as close as the next sentence.

There's an ancient proverb that says, "When the student is ready, the teacher will appear." Maybe there is a teacher waiting for you somewhere down the line. So first, become a meditation student. Establish a steady, daily, 8 minute meditation practice. Then see what unfolds for you.

8. There's Only One Right Way to Meditate.

There is no one way and no best way to meditate. And *caveat emptor:* Be wary of the person, teacher, or school of meditation that tells you different. If they say it's "my way or the highway," stick out your thumb.

Over the next 8 weeks, you'll be introduced to 8 simple meditation techniques. And here's the good news:

- You can do every one of them the first time and every time.

- You won't find a single line of instruction that you can't understand.

- It's impossible to fail at meditation. All you have to do is the best you can, which is what you are doing all the time, whether you know it or not.

So stick around and meditate. After all, how often do you get the opportunity to engage in a win-win situation?

8 MINUTE MEDITATION OPERATING INSTRUCTIONS

These days, everything from bagels to SUVs comes with its own set of operating instructions. These are the instructions you usually *don't* read, and then do whatever the heck you want. Please don't follow this practice with your *8 Minute Meditation* Operating Instructions. They are critical to your meditation practice and as germane to Day One as they will be to Week Eight—and beyond.

Read your operating instructions now. Bookmark this section so you can return whenever you need to. In time, they will naturally incorporate themselves into your meditation practice and operate under your personal radar.

Sit Down and Be Counted

Each time you sit down to meditate, you're standing up for your innate right to peace of mind, self-worth, and happiness.

So when you sit down to meditate, *really sit down! And stay there!* Don't get up for anything—short of a 7.2 earthquake, tsunami, or true emergency. And no, having to pee doesn't qualify as an emergency.

Remember, meditation the 8-minute way is this simple: Nowhere to go. Nothing to do. Nothing to be. Just sitting. For 8 minutes. No more. No less.

Be Kind to Yourself

Not just for the next 8 weeks of the meditation program, but every moment of your life, now and forever.

Frustration frequently arises in the beginning stages of meditation practice. You might become angry at meditation, feeling that it should deliver on some promise that it's not fulfilling.

When anger, confusion, frustration, doubt, embarrassment, or other negative feelings or thoughts arise in meditation, don't be upset or try to repress them. Simply become aware of what is happening. Ask yourself, *In this moment, am I being kind to myself?* And if you are not, do so.

In Week Seven of 8 Minute Meditation, you will learn and do a technique called Lovingkindness Meditation. This practice will aid you in accessing your innate, natural, already-present wellspring of kindness—not just for yourself, but others.

For now, know this: The fact that you have given yourself a meditation practice is a sure sign that you have made a major decision to treat yourself with the kindness and compassion you richly deserve.

8 Minutes. Every Day. No More. No Less.

As your parents told you back in high school, "First graduate. Then you can make your own decisions."

In 8 weeks from now, when you "graduate" from the 8 Minute Meditation program, you'll have a far greater understanding of meditation than you do right now. At that point, you'll be ready to make adjustments to your practice—and, hopefully, upward ones in the number of minutes you meditate. Until that time, though, please stick to the program and meditate for 8 minutes. No more and no less.

Sticking with the program also means that you meditate just

once a day—every day. Don't skip Monday and Tuesday and think you can "make it up" by meditating for twenty-four minutes on Wednesday. That might work when cramming for finals, but it won't work in meditation. Consistency is the cornerstone of a successful meditation practice.

Okay, so now you know exactly how many minutes a day you will meditate for the next eight weeks: 8. There will be plenty of time for tweaking. After graduation.

"Leave the Driving to Us"

I've always loved this classic Greyhound Bus slogan. It's such a perfect way to say "Relax." And I've designed *8 Minute Meditation* so you can do exactly that.

I want you to spend each of your 8 minute meditation periods in meditation, not questioning, doubt, and hesitation. That's why every element of *8 Minute Meditation,* from the Q&As to chapter discussions to the meditation techniques—even these operating instructions—is designed to yield maximum results.

You bought this book because you want to learn to meditate. That is my goal for you. And I'll be there, right alongside you, every step of the way. Not as your guru, but as a supportive coach—and bus driver.

So for the next 8 weeks, relax and feel comfortable in the knowledge that all your needs have been anticipated and taken care of. Trust me, you're going to enjoy the ride.

No Such Thing as a Bad Meditation

The definition of a "good" meditation is "the one you did." The definition of a "bad" meditation is "the one you skipped." So to ensure that you have good meditation every time you meditate, you only have to do one thing, right? Right! Just meditate.

Remember also, in meditation, *failure is impossible*! There is no wrong way to meditate. In fact, the very act of sitting down and meditating, in and of itself, means that you're meditating "correctly."

It's that simple.

Allow . . . Allow . . . Allow

Just as the first rule of real estate is "location, location, location," the first rule of meditation is "allow . . . allow . . . allow."

When you meditate, you allow absolutely everything that arises to arise—and you exclude nothing. This affords you a clear, unobstructed view of the ninety-three-ring circus that is your thinking mind.

Here's how wild that circus can be. In a recent 8 minute meditation session, I dined on a succulent lobster dinner I had in Maine in 1984, heard the theme song from the movie *The Apartment,* and remembered my first two-wheel bicycle (a Rudge). Any connection between these thoughts? If you find it, please let me know.

When you sit down to meditate, your own mind chatter is going to come pouring out. Some thoughts will be pleasant, funny, and blissful. Others might be horrible, depressing, and frightening.

Naturally, you will want to stay with the good stuff and push away the bad stuff.

Don't.

When you meditate, just meditate. Allow every thought, image, and body sensation to "dance its dance." And you just sit this one out.

Please also remember that meditation is not causing your wild displays of mind. The truth is that Roving Mind is always present. The major difference is that, *for the first time in your life,* you're noticing it and dealing with it in a brand-new, better way.

Catch and Release

Catch and release goes hand in hand with "allow . . . allow . . . allow."

In the world of fly fishing, "catch and release" means that after you catch a fish, you unhook it and release it back into the stream. This is exactly what I want you to do with every thought, image, and body sensation that you "hook" during your meditation period.

Your private stream of consciousness is brimming with a lifetime of thoughts, events, and emotions. This means that in every meditation period, you are going to hook thoughts, images, or body sensations that you'll feel compelled to tangle with.

For example, let's say you're meditating, when out of nowhere, the image of the maniac in the huge SUV who cut you off on the highway last evening pops into your mind. Suddenly, you're fantasizing about how you'd like to get even with the driver—devising punishments that would make the Marquis de

Sade cringe! Your body becomes increasingly flushed and feverish. You're seething with rage and righteousness!

What's going on here?

In catch and release terms, you've "hooked" a thought that has now triggered a cascade of other thoughts, images, and body sensations. In a split second, your mind has created a drama that permeates every aspect of your being.

Now, let's run this scenario again, this time using catch and release. Same image of the jerk in the SUV. Same angry thoughts. But now you realize what's going on, and you say to yourself, *Oh, I've hooked onto a thought. I'll just release it.* Which you do, instead of reeling it in, throwing it into your creel, taking it home, scaling, filletting, frying, and eating it.

See how much easier—and wonderful—this is? This simple act of thought releasing is your ticket to freedom—*the freedom* **not** *to engage.* Keep doing this, and allow it to lead you to deeper states of awareness, clarity, and peace in everything you do.

Anglers tell tales about "the one that got away." In meditation, that's not something we regret, but applaud.

Don't Get Mystical-Shmystical

The word *enlightenment* has been bandied about *ad nauseum* in connection with everything from Buddhism to soft drinks. *8 Minute Meditation* is not interested in ideas and discussions of enlightenment and prefers the ancient adage: "Those who say do not know. Those who know do not say."

Meditation is not about experience-hunting for special states of consciousness that go by names such as "enlightenment," "self-realization," or "nirvana." When you meditate, just meditate, without any preconceived notion or agenda about what is going to arise.

Stay open to what comes up and then see what happens. You don't need to name anything.

"Have Fun with It!"

Don't you hate that expression! Still, that has not stopped every teacher in the history of the world from using it, whether they are teaching you to tap dance, mountain-climb, or perform open-heart surgery.

But wait—there's an element of truth here: We usually try so hard to master new skills that we forget about enjoying ourselves in the process. And I want you to enjoy meditating.

Meditation is about *gently allowing* everything that comes in to come in and then gently allowing it to pass on its way. Everything is welcome. Nothing is excluded. And like I said, there is no way you can do it wrong.

So take a deep breath and relax. There's no need to do anything but be. And you can do that, because you've had a lot of practice—your whole life.

So, have fun with it!

Breath Is Home Base

The natural rhythm of your breath is the perfect place to return to whenever you find yourself drawn away from any meditation technique. It's also simple:

- Realize that you have drifted away from your meditation technique.

- Locate the place in your body where your breath is most dominant.

- Direct your attention to that place.

- Take a deep breath, and completely let it go.

- Allow ... allow ... allow.

Breath as home base is a great tool to use anytime during your 8 Minute Meditation program—as well as those other 712 minutes of the day. Try it next time you're in bumper-to-bumper traffic or about to make that important marketing presentation.

In fact, being in touch with your breath is so wonderful and important a technique that I've chosen it for Week One of your 8-week program.

SETUP FOR MEDITATION

Setting up for 8 Minute Meditation is fast, simple, and easy. Here's all you have to do to create a comfortable environment:

- Wear loose-fitting, comfortable clothes that won't constrict your breathing or overheat or chill your body. There are no special meditation robes or garments required.

• Find a quiet room, preferably with a door you can shut for privacy. Adjust the temperature. Slightly cool is preferable.

• Reduce outside distractions as best you can. Don't worry about totally eliminating all noise. It's impossible. Remember: Meditating first thing in the morning or just before bed usually ensures the least outside noise.

• Reduce inside distractions. Turn off the phone, radio, and TV. If you've got family and kids, make a sign to hang on the door, like "Mommy is Meditating. Back in 8 minutes."

• Sit on a comfortable straight-back chair. You don't need any special cushions or mats. The following Q&A section contains simple instructions on posture.

• Set your timing device for 8 minutes. As already mentioned, for best results, use a kitchen timer.

• Review the current week's meditation instructions.

• Start the timer and gently close your eyes.

• Meditate for 8 minutes, until the timer sounds.

Q&A: SETTING UP, GETTING STARTED

Each week of the 8 Minute Meditation program contains a question and answer (Q&A) section. The Q&As aren't here to test you or to see how far you've come. Rather, they are designed to help you over the predictable speed bumps encountered in meditation by everyone, from beginners to masters.

Don't feel embarrassed to go back and consult the Q&As over again. Doing so doesn't mean you're "meditation challenged." On the contrary, it means you're just plain smart. Let's take a look at our first group.

Q: Forget It! I Can't Find 8 Minutes to Meditate— Anywhere or Anytime!

Let me ask you this:

- Are you willing to spend 8 minutes a day to change your life for the better?

- Would you like to spend 8 minutes a day in a calm, peaceful state?

- Would you like to discover a way of being happier in life that doesn't require acquiring something or somebody?

If you answered yes to any of those questions, you can definitely find 8 minutes a day to meditate.

We're not talking about a lot of time here. It's about getting up 8 minutes earlier or going to bed 8 minutes later. A little less of *Good Morning America* or *The Tonight Show*. In exchange for a payoff that could transform your life.

Is it worth it? You know it is. Can you do it? Absolutely!

Q: What Is the Best Time of Day to Meditate?

Upon rising or just before bed.

As already mentioned, it's best to meditate with minimal distraction. Most meditators find that the best time for this is first thing in the morning. That's when the kids are still asleep, the TV isn't blasting, and the phone's not yet ringing. The other best time for meditation is in the evening, just before retiring. The day's done, the kids are in bed, and your home and neighborhood are settled in for the night—unless you live in Brooklyn.

If, for some reason, a different time of the day works better for you, that's fine, too. But remember, *consistency is the hallmark of a strong meditation practice.* No matter what time of the day you chose to meditate, *stick with it on a daily basis.*

Make a standing date with meditation. Show up, and you will never be let down.

Q: Can I Meditate at the Office? A Friend's House? You Know, Catch as Catch Can?

"Catch as catch can" never caught anything.

To say you'll meditate "when I get the chance" or "when I feel like it" is shortchanging meditation—and yourself. The goal here is to establish meditation as a daily habit, such as brushing your teeth. You do that at a certain time and place—in the morning in the bathroom over the sink.

If you meditate in the back of a taxi on the way to the airport on Monday morning, during your lunch break on Tuesday, and at home Wednesday night, you're not establishing a *consistent, daily appointment* with meditation. It's akin to brushing your teeth in a taxicab—something I've rarely seen—or done.

Q: What About Meditation Posture? Don't You Have to Sit Cross-Legged on Some Weird Cushion?

It's not the posture you sit in, but *how you sit in the posture*.

We have all seen those pictures of robe-clad monks in Zen monasteries, sitting silently on low, round cushions (called *zafus*), their legs crossed in full lotus, the traditional sitting posture in this tradition. While this may look peaceful, the truth is that sitting in this position, especially for long periods, is exceedingly uncomfortable—and even painful. Just ask a Zen monk!

8 Minute Meditation does not advocate physical discomfort or pain. When you meditate, you'll sit on a straight-back chair. It may not look as "cool" but it is perfect to get the job done.

Why is posture so important? Correct posture sets the stage for meditation, allowing you to be simultaneously alert yet relaxed.

How can you be both at once? Easy. Just follow these instructions:

8 EASY STEPS FOR CHAIR MEDITATION

1. Place a straight-back chair in a quiet spot with good airflow and minimal intrusion.

2. Slowly lower yourself onto the chair. Wiggle forward on the seat, until you feel your buttock bones two to four inches from the lip of the chair seat. (Note: If you cannot sit with

your back unsupported for 8 minutes, you may lean against the back rest.)

3. Plant your feet directly on the floor and feel the connection. If your feet do not reach completely, place a pillow or blanket underneath them.

4. Gently lower your hands to your lap. You may clasp them or rest one on each thigh.

5. Make sure your head is level. Gaze straight ahead. Keep your spine straight but not jammed. Visualize an imaginary cord attached to the ceiling, extending down and connecting to the top of your head.
6. Relax your jaw. If it feels like it's jutting out, adjust it by gently retracting your chin. If your jaw feels retracted, gently release your chin.

7. Take a deep, relaxed inhale. Slowly allow the exhale. Allow your eyes to gently close.

8. Begin to meditate.

Meditation teacher Sharon Salzberg tells the story of the time she and fellow teacher Joseph Goldstein were seeking a site for what would eventually become the Insight Meditation Society.

The two teachers were in the small town of Barre, Massachusetts, checking out a former monastery that was for sale. The place had great potential but needed a lot of work. As Joseph and Sharon headed into town to brainstorm over lunch, they passed a town police car. Sharon looked over at the door of the police car, which bore Barre's official seal and motto: "Tranquil and Alert." It was at that moment, Sharon says, that she knew she had found the perfect place for a meditation center.

Next time—and every time—you sit down in your meditation posture, remember the Barre town motto: Tranquil and Alert. It's the best posture and meditation instruction I know.

Q: Must I Meditate on an Empty Stomach?

No, but save the pepperoni pizza for later.

There are no hard-and-fast rules about how long you need to wait after a meal before you meditate. Just use your common sense. We all know that a rich meal makes us sleepy. So why go and meditate afterward? You're better off taking a nap or a brisk walk. Give your meal time to digest. Then, when you're feeling more awake, sit down and meditate.

Q: This Technique Isn't Working. Can I Skip It and Try the Next One?

Not a good idea.

Remember the "Leave the Driving to Us" operating instruction? Please follow it. Stick with the technique of the week for the full week before moving on—even if you don't like it. Each week is designed to lead to the next one, gradually bringing you deeper into meditation practice.

8 Minute Meditation was created as a kind of Whitman's Sampler of meditation techniques. You'll taste a new one each

week. After 8 weeks, you'll pick your favorite technique—and stay with that one. You'll see what I mean when you reach Part III.

As far as saying that a meditation technique "isn't working," don't worry. You might not think it is, but it is. There is no need to let Roving Mind indulge in speculation, judgment, or doubt.

So for the next 8 weeks, please follow the program, exactly as it is laid out. This means no switching before it's time.

Q: How Will I Know If I'm Making Progress?

This is a perfectly legitimate concern. After all, we live in a result-oriented society, and when we invest time and effort into something, we want to see progress. In meditation, we measure progress much the same way we would if we were starting a weight training program.

If your goal is to develop your biceps, would you expect, after your first workout, to look in the mirror, flex your arms, and see Popeye staring back? Of course not. Because you know that building physical muscle is a gradual process which requires that you be patient and realistic about seeing progress.

So you keep up your daily workout. For the first several weeks—nothing. But then, one day, you finish your workout, look in the mirror, and—wow!—your biceps pop up like website windows! Aha—progress!

Progress in meditation requires this same kind of patience, commitment, and daily workout. Here, instead of physical muscle, you're building what I call "Mindfulness Muscle." And like building physical muscle, you may not notice it immediately. But one day, you'll sit down to meditate and see that something's changed. Your focus is stronger and steadier, and thoughts slide off you like Teflon. This might be hard to describe, but one thing's for sure: It's *progress*.

Meditators also notice the appearance of Mindfulness Muscle in their daily activities. For example, imagine you're in the supermarket Checkout-Line-From-Hell that never fails to raise your blood pressure. But today, for some reason, you find yourself quiet and content, just relaxing and watching your breath.

Or perhaps you're waiting in front of a movie theater and your date is late. Instead of stifling your anger as you usually do, you find yourself just standing comfortably, allowing all your angry thoughts and feelings to just arise and pass away, like clouds in the sky. By the time your date shows up, you find yourself feeling even better than if he'd arrived on time!

Remember that progress in meditation is both subtle and gradual. Best bet: Don't think about it. When it makes itself known, you'll be the first to know it—and very pleasantly surprised indeed!

Well, finally! We've concluded the preliminaries. There's only one more thing you have to do before you begin your 8 Minute Meditation program: Take the pledge.

THE 8 MINUTE MEDITATION OFFICIAL PLEDGE

Date: _____

I hereby agree with myself that, even if I am traveling, on vacation, under a million family obligations, or have any other "good" excuse not to, I will nevertheless meditate for exactly 8 minutes a day, every day, for the next 8 weeks.

[Escape Clause: If, for some reason, my day is so crazy that I honestly cannot find the time and miss a day, I will continue my meditation program immediately the next day. Note: This escape clause is valid for two uses only!]

(Signed) _____

Congratulations! You're signed up and ready to go. Just turn the page. It's time for Week One of *8 Minute Meditation*. Time to quiet your mind—and change your life.

PART II

• • •

THE 8 WEEK
MEDITATION PROGRAM

LET'S GET DOWN AND MEDITATE!

Time to get down to the real reason you're here. Time to put down the map and discover the territory of meditation.

You've successfully completed Part I. You've read the Meditation Operating Instructions. You know how to correctly sit on your chair. You know how to create your quiet meditation environment. Hey—you already know a lot!

Part II of this book is the heart of *8 Minute Meditation*—the daily, 8 minute regimen you'll be following for the next 8 weeks. It's designed to make meditation simple, easy, pleasant, and part of your daily life.

Part II is divided into eight segments, one for each week of the program. Each segment is broken down into five sections:

• **Where you are.** This is your check-in station. It contains a brief discussion about what might be going on for you at this stage of the 8 Minute Meditation program.

• **What you'll be doing.** This section introduces you to this week's meditation technique.

• **This week's meditation instructions.** These are your clear, simple, step-by-step meditation instructions for the week.

• **How's it going?** Here's where we discuss what might be coming up for you in connection with this week's technique.

• **Q&As.** This weekly section addresses frequently asked questions that arise for meditators.

As you can see, I won't just be saying "ciao" and abandoning you. Nope, I'm here with you for the duration, every step of the way. Who knows, you might even get tired of me! And that is fine—as long as you don't get tired of meditation!

Let's begin Week One.

WEEK ONE

JUST ONE BREATH

WHERE YOU ARE

Welcome to the start of the 8 Minute Meditation program.

Anytime you start something new, questions, doubts, and hopes usually arise. Perhaps you hope that when you sit down to meditate, you'll suddenly become "enlightened," whatever that might mean to you. On the other hand, you might have already decided that meditation is just one more exercise in futility, like the diet you tried last month that didn't work.

All this is, of course, normal, and completely to be expected. And the best way to deal with both positive and negative expectations is to drop them completely. Instead, decide that you will approach this meditation program one minute of meditation at a time.

Today is Day One. By this time next week, you'll have meditated 8 times—which adds up to almost an hour. So ask yourself, *Can I devote an hour of my life to see if I can change my life?*

Sure you can.

WHAT YOU'LL BE DOING: WATCHING YOUR BREATH

The 8 Minute Meditation program commences with the simple yet powerful technique of watching your breath.

I once stayed with a Zen master at his mountaintop monastery in California. His sole teaching instruction was "Just notice breath."

When I heard that, I figured meditation was going to be super-simple, a real no-brainer. So I told him I wanted something a little more challenging, more *macho*. The master smiled knowingly, patted me on the shoulder, and told me to just follow my breath for three breaths. I sat still, closed my eyes, and began.

By the end of my first breath, I had planned the menu for a dinner party four months in the future. By the end of the second, I was figuring out how to make sure my Honda passed the California smog check. And by the end of the third breath—well, you get the picture.

Following your breath may sound simple and easy, like child's play. But, thanks to our constantly Roving Mind, we're anywhere but here. My friend Josh Baran calls this "living in the elsewhere and 'elsewhen'."

But forewarned is forearmed. When (because there is no "if" about this) you are meditating and suddenly find yourself mixing up a batch of brownies or deciding whether to eat Chinese or Italian tonight, just realize that you have strayed off. Then, without judging yourself a "bad" meditator, gently return your awareness to your breath.

This is what breath meditation is about: watching your breath, straying off, realizing it, and gently returning. Over and over again. Like I said, meditation is a practice.

And don't worry, I'll be giving you a lot more detailed meditation instructions than that Zen master gave me.

Let's do it.

THIS WEEK'S MEDITATION INSTRUCTIONS:
JUST ONE BREATH

PREPARATION

- Set your timer for 8 minutes.

- Take your meditation position on your chair, comfortable and alert.

- Gently allow your eyes to close.

- Take a long, deep inhale that sweeps up your current worries, hopes, and dreams. Hold it for a moment. Then gently and slowly "sigh" it out.

- One more time. Deep breath. Release any remaining tension.

- Start your timer.

INSTRUCTIONS

- Notice if you are controlling your breath. If so, release control. Relax.

- Notice that place in your body where you are most aware of the sensation of breathing. It may be your chest, diaphragm, or nostrils. There is no "right" place.

- Gently direct your attention to that place. We call it the "anchor point."

- With your attention on the anchor point, observe the natural rise and fall of the breath. Try to view this as not "your breath" but "*the* breath."

- Allow . . . allow . . . allow. There's no need to become involved or figure anything out.

- Thinking? No problem. Simply notice this. Gently return to your anchor point, your breath.

- Try to follow just one full in-and-out cycle of breath. If you can, then follow another. If you can't, fine. Just start over.

- Frustration? Irritation? Just notice these sensations. And return to your anchor point.

- Continue in this way. Simply observe the natural cycle of breath at your anchor point.

- Can you follow just one breath?

- Do this until your timer sounds.

- Repeat this technique for 8 minutes a day for one week.

HOW'S IT GOING?

Most every meditator feels awkward when they begin to meditate. In fact, I'd be surprised if you didn't feel this way. This can
prompt you to think that maybe you're not cut out to be a meditator. But that isn't true at all.

Consider this: The 8 minutes you just spent in meditation
may be the first time in your life that you've been still, silent, and
awake—simultaneously! Even if you only were like this for two
seconds, it is a radical new way for you to experience the world.
No wonder you feel a little strange.

Learning to meditate is like learning any new skill. At first, you
probably are mentally and physically off-balance. Perhaps you feel
stupid, uncoordinated, even angry—like a real *klutz*. But you stick
it out because you want to do it.

Right now, you may feel weird and awkward. But don't let that
sideline you. Keep up your daily 8 Minute Meditation periods.
One day soon, you'll sit down to meditate and will have what I call
your "aha moment."

When that happens, meditation won't feel strange anymore.
And you'll be glad you stuck around.

Q&A: IN THE BEGINNING

Q: *All I Did Was Think! I Couldn't Stop!*

Of course you couldn't. But don't worry, you're not doing anything wrong.

There's a popular misconception that when you meditate

correctly, all thought ceases. Nothing could be farther from the truth. Meditation is not about *suppressing* thoughts, but *surpassing* them.

Accept this reality: It is your mind's job to think—24/7. And it's not going to stop just because you sit down for 8 minutes and tell it to "Shut up, already!" But the good news is this: When you stop trying to stop your thoughts, you begin to surpass them. *This can lead you to the peace you thought you could only achieve when you stopped thinking!*

Now would be a good time to go back and reread the "Catch and Release" and "Allow … Allow … Allow" Operating Instructions. They'll remind you how to approach and deal with Roving Mind.

Also, try my Meditator's "ABC": **A**lways **B**e **C**alm. That's a good mnemonic device, for meditation and everything else in your life, no matter what arises.

Q: Why Do I Feel So Restless Just Sitting Still?

Along with a restless mind, a restless body is the most common challenge beginning meditators encounter. It's also perfectly normal and understandable.

In breath meditation, we sit still and do nothing but neutrally observe the breath. We try not to engage in give-and-take with Roving Mind, which doesn't appreciate this lack of attention. To get our attention back, Roving Mind sends signals to the body, urging it to "Don't just sit there. Do something!"

I encourage you to do exactly the opposite: *"Don't just do something. Sit there."* As you develop your meditation practice, your mind and body will gradually acclimate to being still. In the beginning, this might take up almost your entire 8 minute meditation period. But even if you experience only seven seconds of focus, it is very significant.

One day, you will find that your mind will, of its own accord, settle down quickly, perhaps only a minute or so into your meditation period, or even as you take your preparation breaths. As for your body, it will eventually, of its own accord, head for peace like a homing pigeon.

Q: I'm Not Meditating Correctly. Am I?

Every beginning meditator believes he or she is meditating wrong. Not true. As I've already said, no matter how you meditate, you're always doing it correctly. Here's what may be happening to make you believe you're not:

You sit down to meditate and, of course, your mind begins to wander. You believe that you must be doing something wrong or this wouldn't be happening. Perhaps a part of your body, your right foot for example, suddenly feels uncomfortable. Or you realize that you need to use the restroom. So now you've got your mind straying, your foot aching, and your bladder about to burst! And you think *Meditation is supposed to make me peaceful. And it's not! This can't be right!*

But it *is* right. And you only have to do one thing: *Allow exactly what is coming up to come up.* It's your resistance to "what is" that is causing you to feel that things are wrong.

Once you begin to allow and accept exactly what is going on, you can stop battling with your thoughts and feelings and surrender to them.

When you begin to allow your thoughts, feelings, and emotions to just do their thing, something magical happens: They don't bother you! They become like puffy clouds, scudding across a limitless sky. And you are that sky.

Next time you wonder if you're meditating correctly, stop and answer this question: *Did I, for 8 minutes, try my best to do today's meditation technique?* (Notice that this is about trying, not being perfect.)

Of course you did! Congratulations! You just meditated right. Keep it up.

Q: What Can I Do If I Feel Scary Thoughts and Feelings When I Meditate?

Don't be afraid of being afraid.

Feelings of fear and disorientation are common in meditation, whether you are a beginner or master. By the way, so are feelings of bliss, peace, and love. But let's look at the uncomfortable ones and why they might be arising.

The practice of meditation can free your body and mind in a whole new way, propelling thoughts, feelings, and emotions up from deep within to the surface of awareness, just as bubbles rise from the bottom of a glass of club soda. Some of these thoughts and memories can be unsettling and frightening, especially ones we never knew we had or might have unknowingly suppressed.

Instead of resisting and suppressing these thoughts, deal with them exactly how you deal with everything in meditation. Allow them to arise, do their thing, and then float off.

Go back and review the "Catch and Release" Operating Instruction. Also remember that in meditation, we handle mind, emotional, and body states this way:

- If you like it, don't go running after it.

- If you don't like it, don't run away from it.

This is a good rule of thumb, not just for meditation, but for life.

Q: Should I Be Trying Harder To Meditate?

Alan Watts, the well-known meditation teacher, wrote that it was impossible to meditate. What he meant by that statement was this: You can't try to meditate and be meditating at the same time. In other words, meditation is something you need to allow to happen on its own.

Remember when you first learned how to swim? In the beginning you struggled mightily to keep your head above water. But then, one day, something amazing happened: You gave up fighting to stay afloat. And when you did, you rose to the surface and floated effortlessly.

Meditation is like this. You are immersed in a sea of your own thoughts, body sensations, and feelings, struggling against them. Until the moment when you remember to just "allow ... allow ... allow" them. And when you do, when you surrender into what is, you find yourself floating effortlessly in serenity.

Q: Meditation Is Incredibly Boring. Nothing's Happening!

Actually, a lot is happening when you meditate, but in a different way than you may be used to.

There's a great *New Yorker* cartoon by Gahan Wilson in which a meditation student sits across from his master, who is irritated with the question the student has just asked: "What happens next?" The master roars, "*Nothing* happens next!"

But this "nothing" is really a big "something." When you drop your expectation of what meditation is and how it is supposed to change you—when you let go of *everything* and just sit quietly and peaceably for 8 minutes—you create the environment for movement to occur. And your life starts to change.

So, if only for the 8 minutes a day you meditate, allow all notions and expectations about what you think is supposed to happen to drop away. In time, you will see that the "nothing happens next" might just be the biggest "something" that ever happened to you!

Q: Should My Eyes Be Open or Closed When I Meditate?

It varies according to the meditation teacher, technique, and tradition.

One meditation technique called Yogic Skygazing has you keep your eyes as wide open as possible. The Vipassana and Insight Meditation traditions have you close your eyes. Zen practitioners half-close their eyes and gaze down.

In the *8 Minute Meditation* program, you keep your eyes

closed. And although this can be very relaxing, it does not mean that it's time for you to "space out" or take a nap. In fact, just the opposite is true.

Remember the Stanley Kubrick film title, *Eyes Wide Shut?* This is a good reminder that, in meditation, even though your physical eyes are shut, your "mind's eye" remains wide open and alert. Here are two pointers on how to do this:

- Don't squeeze your eyes shut. Allow them to close gently and naturally.

- Keep the eyes "soft." Relax your focus.

After Week Four of the meditation program, you're welcome to experiment with Zen eye position:

Soften your eyes, and let your gaze drop to a forty-five-degree angle with the floor. Gently allow your eyelids to close until they are about one-third open.

If this works better for you than eyes closed, continue this way. If not, go back to closing your eyes.

Either way, remember that closing your eyes in meditation isn't about losing awareness but gaining it.

You're doing great! If this is your seventh day, turn
the page and move on to next week.

NAKED SOUND

WHERE YOU ARE

Congratulations! You've successfully completed Week One of 8 Minute Meditation!

You've made your desire to learn to meditate a reality, maybe for the first time in your life. At this point, you've meditated for almost an hour. If you have never meditated before, this is a new personal record. And by this time next week, you'll have doubled it.

Last week we worked with breath meditation. And I'm sure your (and everyone's) constant companion—Roving Mind—frequently interrupted your meditation periods. You may have also had the experience, if only for a moment, of Roving Mind disappearing and your thoughts passing by like clouds across an open sky.

This is a taste of meditation, an insight into how meditation allows you to stay peaceful and calm, no matter what thoughts your mind churns out.

If you don't think you had this experience, don't worry, because at some point you will. It's a natural outgrowth of meditation practice.

As you prepare for Week Two, this would be a good time to review several important operating instructions:

- **Allow ... allow ... allow.** Allow whatever comes up. And exclude nothing. Emotions, thoughts, images—they're all treated equally. The more you completely accept them, the more present you are and the more fluid your meditation.

- **Catch and release.** When you realize that you've hooked onto a thought, gently unhook and release it. Over time, you'll become much more skillful at noticing when you've "hooked" something. After a while, releasing will become easier and more automatic.

Keep this dynamic duo in mind as you begin Week Two. And remember, by this time next week, you'll have fourteen—count 'em—fourteen meditation sessions under your belt.

So without further ado, onward.

WHAT YOU'LL BE DOING

Don't worry. Naked Sound Meditation doesn't mean you'll be disrobing. It's my way of describing a way to meditate that anchors you in the coming and going of sound, without needing to know what it is, what it means, or where it's coming from.

Noise pollution has reached epidemic proportions. We live at the mercy of a constant assault from blaring stereos, shrieking car alarms, droning airplane engines, and ear-splitting emergency vehicle sirens.

You most likely get your daily earful of noise pollution and have probably invented your own formula to shut it out. This usually involves the creation and application of physical and psychological "earmuffs."

For example, construction site next door driving you bonkers? Turn up the stereo. Kids making too much noise? Vodka martini to the rescue. Car alarm that won't stop squawking? Stereo *and* martini!

These tactics may work, but only up to a point. And there's a much better way: meditation. Believe it or not, meditation can help you handle noise pollution—no earmuffs required. That's what Naked Sound Meditation is all about.

Naked Sound Meditation is a technique that treats sound in all its pristine nakedness. For the next week, you'll spend 8 minutes a day just hearing sounds—without defining, filtering, rejecting, or judging them. You'll be amazed at how profoundly relaxing this can be.

Here's an illustration of what I mean: You're meditating. Suddenly, in the background, you hear a faint drone that starts to become louder. Before you're even aware of it, your mind has identified it as a small airplane. And a series of thoughts, images, and body sensations follows close behind like foot soldiers. It might go something like this:

Damn, I hate that plane! It's interfering with my meditation. It sounds much too close. The pilot is an idiot! I'm an idiot! I never should have moved this close to the airport. I wish I had enough money to move to the country.

Get the picture? It starts with a simple, neutral, buzzing sound. Next thing you know, you've upset yourself. This is an example of Roving Mind just doing its job, which is to constantly receive, analyze, and *associate* all sensory input, not only with hearing, but with all five senses.

But there is another less stressful and more skillful option.

Imagine yourself once again in meditation. Here comes that plane. You hear the buzzing drone: louder . . . louder . . . louder . . . louder. But that's all you do. Just hear it. Not as a plane, but as *just sound*. Allow that sound to just be what it is and do what it does. In a few moments, the sound, of its own accord, begins fading . . . fading . . . fading . . .

And that's it. Sound came. Sound went. It did its dance and moved on. *You didn't dance with it, latch onto it, push it away, or tell a story about it.* This is what I call "naked sound": sound unembellished by your concepts, associations, and images.

Naked Sound Meditation might appear simple, but don't be surprised when you encounter difficulty with it. Consider the preceding example and how instantaneously the mind needs to associate sounds with judgments, thoughts, and beliefs. Expect this to occur once, if not many times, when you meditate.

And don't worry, get upset, or think you're doing things wrong. Just keep on keeping on. This is why we call meditation a practice.

Turn the page, and let's begin.

THIS WEEK'S MEDITATION INSTRUCTIONS:
NAKED SOUND

PREPARATION

- Set your timer for 8 minutes.

- Take your meditation position on your chair, comfortable and alert.

- Gently allow your eyes to close.

- Take a long, deep inhale that sweeps up your current worries, hopes, and dreams. Hold it for a moment. Then gently and slowly "sigh" it out.

- One more time. Deep breath. Release any remaining tension.

- Start your timer.

INSTRUCTIONS

- Bring your attention to the sounds around you. All sounds. Without filtering or rejecting them.

- Allow these sounds to rise and fall of their own accord. As they do, just note them by silently saying the words *rising* or *falling*.

- Be with each sound completely. If one sound rises as another falls, see if you can give both equal attention, noting their individual "rising" and "falling."

- A sound is just a sound. There is no need to match it to an object.

- If a sound does give rise to a thought image or body sensation—no problem. Simply notice this. Gently return to your meditation on just allowing sound to rise and fall.

- Do this until your timer sounds.

- Repeat this technique for 8 minutes a day for one week.

HOW'S IT GOING?

Although you most likely found Naked Sound Meditation challenging, you also hopefully got a taste of how peaceful it can be when you just allow things to be the way they are. So why not try and apply the Naked Sound technique to your other senses, for a complete experience of sight, taste, smell, and touch.

How can you do this? Here's an example of how to convert Naked Sound to "Naked Sight":

It's spring, and you happen upon a beautiful cherry tree bursting with blossoms. You stop, become quiet, and simply look at the tree. You don't compare it with the cherry tree you saw last year in Washington, D.C. or judge it against apple blossoms down the road. Instead, you "just see" exactly the same way you "just listened" to sounds in Naked Sound—without ideas, thoughts, judgments, or comparisons.

When you look at a tree this way, it's like seeing nature for the first time. The experience can be joyful, even overwhelming. Imagine going through your day like this, just seeing, just eating, just smelling, just feeling, without filtering, criticism, or judgment.

Sound wonderful? It is. And meditation can help you be this way.

Q&A: AM I MEDITATING CORRECTLY?

Q: My Meditation Session Was Bad. What's Wrong?

You'll never hear anyone complain when they've had a "good" meditation session. But if it's a "bad" one, oh boy, watch out! Right away, you figure something must be terribly wrong! Here's a typical mind scenario:

Okay, I'm meditating . . . Following instructions perfectly . . . I'm supposed to be serene, happy, and blissful! . . . And I definitely am not! . . . I'll never get the hang of it! . . . This is a bad meditation!

If this sounds familiar, relax. Not only is this not a bad meditation session, it's a *perfect* one. Why? Because it shows you that the problem isn't with your meditation, but with your judging mind, which in this case has decided that this meditation period is bad.

As you know from the Meditation Operating Instructions, the only criterion as to whether a meditation period was good or bad is this: "A good meditation is the one you did. A bad meditation is the one you skipped." Keep that in mind.

And keep meditating. It's all *good*.

Q: How Do I Know This Meditation Technique Is Right for Me?

There are hundreds of meditation techniques to choose from. Once you complete the 8 week meditation program, you'll be in a much better position to seek out and choose techniques that resonate perfectly with you. But for just this time, allow me to choose for you.

It's important that you follow the program the way it's presented and give each meditation technique a full seven-day trial period. This will hopefully discourage the growth of the widespread affliction I call "Contentment Shopping"—something that results in anything *but* contentment.

Contentment Shopping is the nonstop, acquisitive quest for "something" out there that will make us happy. You know, that thing that you just have to have, no matter what. Here's how it works:

You see an item, anything from a $2.99 bag of Hershey bars to a $89,000 BMW. You think *If I can just have that, I'll be happy.* Then you do whatever you have to do to get it. And you're happy—for a brief moment. Which would be about two minutes for the Hershey bars. And for the BMW, a lot longer—up to two whole weeks, or until the first ding in the fender.

Your desire to switch to another meditation technique is just another version of the Hershey bars and the BMW. You believe that if you can get a different meditation technique, your meditation problems will be over, and you'll be happy. On the other hand, if you commit to staying with the meditation technique, even for one week, it could be a meaningful step towards freeing yourself from the belief that happiness is somewhere "out there," in the next thing. It could be the first break in the vicious cycle of Contentment Shopping. Doesn't this sound like a better choice?

So stick with this week's meditation technique until it's time for change. Notice all the questions and doubts that tell you there's a better meditation technique out there. And if you could just have that one . . .

Q: How Will I Know If Meditation Is "Working"?

The way meditation works is different from the way other things work. *What seems to be happening* and *what is really happening* when you meditate are two different things.

Let's say you've just sat down to meditate. At this point you feel, well, like you're just sitting there, like a bump on a log. Next thing you know, you're experiencing a nonstop stream of thoughts, feelings, and body sensations—some of which might have to do with meditation, like how you're doing it wrong or that it's a waste of time. But that's not true: A powerful process is at work here, flying below your radar.

I've already discussed how meditation builds "Mindfulness Muscle" and how every 8 minute meditation period you complete contributes to building that muscle. This is going on whenever you meditate *whether you are aware of it or not.*

Knowing this frees you. You don't need to keep monitoring yourself for results. All you have to do is simply follow the 8 Minute Meditation program. It's working, whether you know it or not.

Q: I Fell Asleep While I Was Meditating. Is That Okay?

It's fine. Now it's time to meditate.

Every meditator, at some point, falls asleep on the job. You go into a relaxed state and—bye, bye. There's nothing wrong with falling asleep, and you need never chastise and berate yourself for doing so.

On the other hand, your snooze doesn't count as your meditation period. The best thing to do when you wake up is—you guessed it—set your timer for 8 minutes—and begin again to meditate.

Here are a few simple things that can help you stay awake and alert when you meditate:

• Maintain correct sitting posture. It's important that you sit straight and upright. It's when you start slouching that you doze off. This simple correction can make a huge difference in wakefulness. Dozing off is always a good reminder to go back and review the posture instructions in Part I.

• Keep your room a tad on the cool side. Turn off the heat. Let in some fresh air. Remove sweaters, vests, or scarves.

• Splash a little cool water on your face before you sit down to meditate.

• Do some short physical exercise to get your circulation going. Just several deep breaths can do wonders.

• Never meditate right after a heavy meal, a triple espresso, or a glass of champagne.

• Don't make meditation time nap time. You've already defeated your own purpose.

You're doing great! If this is your seventh day,
turn the page and move on to next week.

NOTING BODY SENSATIONS

WHERE YOU ARE

Congratulations. You've got fourteen days of meditation practice under your belt! As a famous meditation master once said, "Everything's perfect! And there's always room for improvement."

At this point in the program, you may find yourself:

- Settling down into meditation more easily

- More relaxed and less awkward with meditation

- Starting to see that meditation isn't too hard—nor too easy

- Impatient that you're not progressing as fast as you might have expected

The first three items aren't problematic. In fact, they indicate progress. But let's take a look at the last one: impatience.

Right now, please take a long, deep, slow breath. Good. Now you're ready to read on.

Impatience is a common feeling that comes up in the beginning stage of meditation practice and usually arises either because:

• You are enjoying meditation. You want to get even better at it—right now!

• You aren't enjoying meditation. You feel frustrated and irritated. You want meditation to "kick in"—right this instant!

These seemingly opposing viewpoints are actually the flip side of the same coin, called "expectation." These strong preferences provide a good opportunity for observation when they surface during meditation. Notice these thoughts, feelings, and emotions as they arise, and apply the "Catch and Release" and "Allow . . . Allow . . . Allow" Operating Instructions.

This week you're going to add something new to your meditation toolbox. It's a technique called "Noting Body Sensations." It's a fresh, new way to explore terrain that you think you really know—your body. I think you'll be in for an eye-opener.

Let's do it.

WHAT YOU'LL BE DOING

There's an old movie called *Fantastic Voyage* that starred Raquel Welch and Stephen Boyd. The two of them, clad in tight jumpsuits (I wonder why?), are miniaturized and then proceed to pilot a micro-scopic space shuttle through the bloodstream of the president, try-ing to find a blood clot in his brain before it's too late—which, if course, it isn't.

Week Three of your 8 Minute Meditation program is going to take you on your own fantastic voyage of sorts: inside your own body. Jumpsuits are optional.

The meditation technique you'll do this week is called "Not-ing." Noting is a simple yet powerful technique that enables you to focus your attention.

Here's a brief preview of noting. Try this now:

- Take a deep breath and gently close your eyes.

- Relax into your body. Really allow yourself to occupy it.

- Are you drawn to a prominent sensation somewhere, in-ternally or externally?

- Good. Note where it is. You need not label the exact body part or area where the sensation is located.

- Observe the sensation without analysis or judgment. Just watch.

As you can see, you need not be concerned with the exact location of the prominent body sensation. The only thing you need to do is sense the sensation, note it, and direct your aware-ness to it.

A brief word about difficulty: You might find noting more challenging than the previous techniques you've done with breath and sound. That's because your "anchor point" in noting meditation is not centered in one place, but instead is in constant motion throughout your body. Don't feel frustrated if you find it a challenge. Noting is well worth your exploration and can "turbocharge" your level of awareness. Remember that you're building Mindfulness Muscle here.

Okay, it's time to fasten your seatbelt, and take off—on your own fantastic voyage.

THIS WEEK'S MEDITATION INSTRUCTIONS:
NOTING

PREPARATION

- Set your timer for 8 minutes.

- Take your meditation position on your chair, comfortable and alert.

- Gently allow your eyes to close.

- Take a long, deep inhale that sweeps up your current worries, hopes, and dreams. Hold it for a moment. Then gently and slowly "sigh" it out.

- One more time. Deep breath. Release any remaining tension.

- Start your timer.

INSTRUCTIONS

- Allow your body to relax. Notice the different body sensations that arise. Do this for a few moments.

- At some point, you will feel an area in your body sort of "light up."

- Note this place. It is not necessary to label this body part.

- Bring your awareness to this dominant area. And rest your attention there. This is your current anchor point.

- Soon, a new area of sensation will light up. Treat it as you did the first area. Make it your current anchor point. Note this new area and rest your attention here. Allow it. Observe it. Do nothing about it or to it.

- When thoughts arise, just notice them. No need to get involved. Gently return to the place where you sense your dominant body sensation.

- Repeat this technique for 8 minutes a day for one week.

HOW'S IT GOING?

Now that you've had a chance to experience noting meditation, here's a fun way to better understand what this meditation is all about. Let's take a little sojourn back to the heyday of TV and that famous cop show, *Dragnet*.

If you recall, on the show, Jack Webb played the laconic,

stone-faced LAPD Sergeant Joe Friday. And you could rest assured that at some point in each episode, Sgt. Friday would wind up interrogating a female witness to a crime. During that scene, he would never fail to utter his famous line: "Just the facts, ma'am."

What Friday meant by this was that his *only* concern was with the bare bones of the event—the pure, unadulterated facts, the exactly-what-happened. He wasn't interested in what the witness thought, imagined, or wished she saw. All Sarge wanted were the facts, ma'am. Period.

"Just the facts" is also how I want you to approach all your meditation techniques. Here's what I mean:

- When you're noting a body sensation, just note it.

- When you're watching your breath, just watch it.

- When you hear a sound, just hear it.

The operative—and crucial—word is *just*. As this "just-ness" begins to permeate and saturate your awareness more and more, your meditation practice can take you to a new place of allowing and balance, where you're more relaxed and open, not just to meditation—but your entire life.

And *that's* a fact.

Q&A: THINKING, THINKING, THINKING . . .

Q: What Do I Do with Unwanted Thoughts That Appear During Meditation?

Do exactly the *opposite* of what you usually do.

Our waking lives overflow with a nonstop litany of human emotions that run the gamut from pure bliss to unadulterated hell. The way we normally deal with thoughts is to give them a lot more credit than they deserve, thinking that we are obligated to follow them wherever they lead us.

As the cliché says, "One thought leads to another." And that's exactly what happens, over and over again, *ad infinitum*—and *ad nauseum*. Exhausting, isn't it? What can you possibly do to rest your weary mind and get some peace? Meditate.

Meditation is the antidote to Roving Mind. All you have to do is—well, nothing. Here's how:

- A thought arises. You watch it, allow it, and release it.

- A new thought arises. You watch it, allow it, and release it.

- Another thought arises. Guess what? Exactly! You watch it, allow it, and release it.

If you think this sounds a lot like the "Allow . . . Allow . . . Allow" and "Catch and Release" Operating Instructions you're exactly right. And that's good news, because you don't have to learn anything new. Just keep doing what you've been doing.

By now, you are starting to realize that thoughts always arise during meditation, no matter how calm and relaxed you are or how proficient a meditator you become. But the good news is that you are also starting to develop an immunity to the lure of Roving Mind—no matter how seductive it seems.

Remember your operating instructions and our definition of meditation. Allow what is. Rest your weary mind. Bask in the peace you deserve.

Q: I'm Having More Thoughts Than Ever Since I Started Meditating. Why Is Meditation Causing This?

As Garcia said, just before he delivered dire battle news to his commander, "Don't kill the messenger!"

There's an enormous difference between noticing thoughts more and noticing more thoughts. In meditation, it's the former, not the latter, that's happening, even if it doesn't seem that way.

Meditation does not produce an increase in thinking, but rather makes you *realize*, for the first time in your life, how much thinking you actually do. This is something you probably never noticed before. So instead of concluding that meditation is messing up your mind, be grateful for this new realization.

Next time you meditate and the thought comes up that "Meditation is causing more thoughts," treat it exactly how you're learning to treat all your thoughts: with allowance and nonengagement. It's another perfect opportunity to deal with Roving Mind in an infinitely more skillful—and peaceful—way.

Q: While Meditating, I Had a Moment Where I Felt I Was Really Here. It Felt Wonderful, Then It Was Gone. How Do I Get It Back?

What you might have experienced was a natural state that is your birthright. It has many names, but for the moment, let's call it "presence." It's life itself, without the overlay of your nonstop "I" machine that continually obscures it from view.

Presence is always right here and available to you, in every moment. But the only way you can return to presence is, paradoxically, not to try to return to it. To help you better understand what I mean, try this:

- Stop whatever you're doing.

- Review the thoughts you've had over the past five minutes. Don't worry if you can't remember most of them.

- What percentage of your thoughts would you say involved planning your future? Or remembering your past?

- Where were "you" when you were thinking these thoughts?

Even just a few minutes of observation demonstrates how much of your waking life is spent in either the dead past or the nonexistent future. It's amazing how seldom in the day you are actually present, in this very moment, which is the most wonderful place you can ever be.

Here's where meditation can help. Even though you can't decide to be in presence, meditation can allow you to become what

Catherine Ingram, teacher and author of the book *Passionate Presence,* calls "more presence-prone." How? By going, as Catherine puts it, "upstream from thought."

As you continue to meditate, you can spend more time upstream, and this place becomes more pronounced and intimate. You begin to understand, on a nonintellectual level, that presence is not something that comes from "out there" and has just randomly—and temporarily—dropped in for a visit. Instead, you come to realize presence as your natural inner state—always here and always available, in the silent space accessed through meditation.

Q: When I Meditated, My Mind Kept Singing "White Christmas" Over and Over Again. It's Maddening. What Do I Do?

Don't worry, you're not going crazy. The appearance of popular songs, commercial jingles, and school alma maters during meditation is a very common occurrence.

Let's say it's December, and you're in the midst of your 8 Minute Meditation period. Suddenly your mind begins to play a familiar melody. It's the Irving Berlin classic, "White Christmas" and the voice of course, is that of Bing Crosby.

But once isn't enough! It's as if there's an old phonograph record grafted into your brain, playing the song over and over again. You try to banish it from your mind, but as usual, the harder you try, the more persistently it stays.

Your reaction to this intrusion is probably less than skillful, somewhere along the lines of *Oh, for crying out loud! Get lost! Can't you see I'm meditating?* But do Irving and Bing care? Absolutely not!

What in the world do you do so that you can keep meditating? Here's what:

To adapt a line from Gertrude Stein: "A thought is a thought is a thought." Remember your Catch and Release Operating Instruction? What's happened here is that you've hooked onto a thought, in the form of a series of words that make up a song. All you need to do is treat the song as you would a single thought: Gently unhook it and release it back into the stream.

May your days be merry and bright.

You're doing great! If this is your seventh day,
turn the page and move on to next week.

THIS MAGIC MOMENT ☉

WHERE YOU ARE

You're about to begin your fourth week of meditation practice. By now, you've meditated for almost three hours! Amazing! Give yourself a huge pat on the back.

Right about now, you may be having one or more of the following experiences:

• You're getting cozier with meditation. It's like wrapping yourself in a warm, welcoming comforter, something you want to do every day.

• You're more accepting of your thoughts and body sensations, even the unpleasant ones. *Terra incognita* is becoming more familiar.

• You're beginning to understand the temporary and fleeting nature of your emotions, body sensations, and thinking. They arise by themselves and eventually float off like clouds.

• You're becoming more adept at letting go of whatever arises in meditation, be they thoughts, images, or body sensations. Catch and release is becoming an automatic part of your being.

This is splendid progress, and you are to be congratulated for your dedication and willingness to stay with the program. Let's move on to Week Four.

WHAT YOU'LL BE DOING

This week's meditation technique is, once again, about being present in this moment. And to enable you to do that, you'll be working with the technique I call "This Magic Moment."

We discussed "presence" in last week's Q&As. You might want to review it again before reading on.

Presence is simply about *being here now,* which might seem a bit absurd to you. *What's the big deal?* you might say, *I'm always here now. Where else could I possibly be?*

Fair question. So let's take a moment and find out if you really are here now. I'd like you to stop reading and put down this book.

Then, take a deep breath, gently allow your eyes to close, and completely relax and allow your next four cycles of breath.

Okay, open your eyes and answer this: Were you completely present for those four breaths? By this, I mean were you *right here*? Or was your mind coming up with thoughts like *Why am I sitting here with my eyes closed?* or *Is this what he means by being 'present'?* Take a good look at what happened.

This exercise illustrates that although you live under the assumption that you're "here" all the time, the truth is quite the contrary: You are "here" a lot *less* than you know. And "there" a lot *more* than you know.

This Magic Moment Meditation is all about bringing you into the elusive present. Let's begin.

THIS WEEK'S MEDITATION INSTRUCTIONS:
THIS MAGIC MOMENT

PREPARATION

- Set your timer for 8 minutes.

- Take your meditation position on your chair, comfortable and alert.

- Gently allow your eyes to close.

- Take a long, deep inhale that sweeps up your current worries, hopes, and dreams. Hold it for a moment. Then gently and slowly "sigh" it out.

- One more time. Deep breath. Release any remaining tension.

- Start your timer.

INSTRUCTIONS

- Relax and allow your mind to settle.

- A thought arises. It is most likely about the past or the future.

- Label the thought either "past" or "future."

- Allow the thought to go its way, to do its dance.

- As the thought moves off, notice the space around it. Silent. Still. Here. Now.

- Surrender into this silent, vast presence.

- Another thought arises. Don't resist it. Again, just label it "past" or "future."

- Is your mind wandering off into thoughts, body sensations, or emotions? No problem. Just notice them and allow them to float away, like clouds in a boundless sky.

- Allow thoughts. Allow silence. Allow everything.

- Do this until your timer sounds.

- Repeat this technique for 8 minutes a day for one week.

HOW'S IT GOING?

This Magic Moment is designed to help you understand, on a non-intellectual level, the difference between being here, as opposed to elsewhere and "elsewhen."

A good illustration of this is to be found in a cartoon that appeared in *The New Yorker* magazine (which seems to have a thing for monks!). Here's the setup:

A Zen monk, smiling beatifically, perches on his meditation cushion in the difficult cross-legged full lotus position. A cartoon "thought balloon" floats above his head. And what's inside that balloon?

A chair!

Besides being funny, this cartoon expresses the truth that, no matter how seasoned the meditator, it doesn't take much to drag him completely out the moment, no matter how he might appear to the world. Our cartoon monk has most likely been sitting motionless for hours in an uncomfortable posture. His inability to accept his discomfort has sent him into the remembered past (*Gee, remember how good sitting in a chair felt?*) or the imagined future (*Gee, wouldn't a chair be great?*). Or both!

Each one of us is this cartoon monk, dreaming of sitting in a chair that is somewhere else—instead of being right here, where we are. One of the great blessings of meditation is that it affords us, perhaps for the first time, a calm place to observe the mind's incessant search for that elusive something that will make things right.

This understanding, gained through meditation, can lead to a new sense of personal freedom and peace.

Q&A: MUSIC, MANTRAS, NOISE, AND INCENSE

Q: I've Been Told That Listening to Music Enhances Meditation. Can I Play My Favorite Music When I Meditate?

It's best not to. Here's why:

When you meditate, you want to create as level a playing field as possible—maybe even tilted a bit in your favor. One way to achieve this is to minimize outside distractions. Playing any type of music while you meditate not only creates unnecessary noise, but also triggers associations and memories of what the song or music means. These conscious and unconscious thoughts practically guarantee that you will be pulled away from your meditation.

Why make it tougher on yourself? Keep as level a playing field as possible. Save the music for later. You'll enjoy it more, too.

Q: Can I Burn Incense While I Meditate?

No smoking—for the next 8 minutes.

The reasoning here is the same as the one for music: The smell of incense can distract you from the main event—meditation. It's like being a cliff diver, perched on a cliff 300 feet above the Pacific, who says, "Y'know, this isn't hard enough. So I'll just blindfold myself and spin around like a *piñata* before I dive."

Again, keep your meditation playing field as level as possible. Wait until you've finished your meditation session to light up your joss sticks, scented candles, aromatherapy lamps—or anything your heart desires. You'll appreciate those pleasant scents even more because you'll be more present to smell them.

Q: It's Too Noisy to Meditate, No Matter How Many Windows I Close.

It's never "too anything" to meditate.

Noise pollution is epidemic today. Unless your current mailing address is a mountaintop in Nepal, a hearing test booth, or the moon, chances are 100% that unwanted sound and noise surround you. But this doesn't mean you can't meditate. In fact, unwanted noise can lead to a deeper meditative experience because it forces you to get more creative.

As I've said, before you sit down to meditate, make your best effort to minimize noise. Close your windows, shut off the radio or TV, subdue children and spouses, and wait for the gardener to finish mowing the lawn. Once you've done all you can do, then just sit down and meditate, accepting the fact that unwanted noise will likely intrude into your space.

It's rare to have a completely noise-free meditation session. For instance, you might wait until everyone has gone to bed and the house is silent. You sit down to meditate. And *whaa!* ... there goes that car alarm. Or your neighbor's cat. Or your baby.

When this happens, turn that noise into an opportunity to deepen your meditation practice. Switch to Naked Sound and just hear the noise as noise. Don't label, criticize, analyze, or judge it. Practice with Naked Sound for the remainder of your meditation period. You can always return to your current technique tomorrow.

Meditation can help you develop a new way of dealing with unwanted noise. Allow it to rise, fall, and disappear. The more you let go of noise, the less it will annoy you.

Q: Speaking of Sound, I Saw This PBS Special Where Monks Were Chanting Something Called a "Mantra." What Is It? And Can I Do That Instead?

Simply put, *mantra* is a meditation practice in the Buddhist and other traditions in which the practitioner focuses on repeating a certain sound, word, phrase, or prayer. Repetition of the word "Om" is one of the most universally popular mantras.

8 Minute Meditation is designed to be unobtrusive, allowing you to meditate anywhere, without disturbing anyone else. Mantras are usually chanted out loud, often as loudly as possible. This can not only disturb others, but also draw unnecessary attention to you. Not a great idea.

After you complete your 8 week meditation program, feel free to explore mantra or any other meditation tradition you fancy. But for now, and the remainder of this program, please recall—and follow—the "Leave the Driving to Us" Operating Instruction.

You're doing great! If this is your seventh day,
turn the page and move on to next week.

GRACIOUS DECLINING

WHERE YOU ARE

Congratulations! You're halfway through the 8 Minute Meditation program and into your fifth week as a meditator. At this point, you've got thirty-two meditation periods under your belt. That's 192 minutes—more than 3 hours of meditation. You are doing incredibly well.

This week we'll be exploring a meditation technique I call "Gracious Declining." It's a technique that will allow you to further develop your skill in the art of "meeting and greeting" pesky thoughts.

I've already said it, but it's definitely worth repeating: There is nothing intrinsically wrong with thinking. You need a sound, working mind to survive, do your job, provide for your family, and remember which toothbrush in the rack is yours. This is not the kind of thinking I'm talking about. It's the other kind—the useless, negative thinking that clutters and clogs your awareness, keeping you from living in peace.

If you've been paying attention to your incessant mind stream these past four weeks, you've probably noticed something striking: Useful, vital, and essential thoughts make up only a tiny part of your thinking. It's the useless, unhelpful, and oftentimes painful thoughts that predominate.

Gracious Declining is a technique that can help you develop a skillful new way to deal with your mind clutter. All that's required is that you be firm and polite.

WHAT YOU'LL BE DOING

The Gracious Declining meditation technique is designed to help you nip rambling thought streams in the bud. Here's an illustration of what I mean:

Imagine your thoughts as an endless line of salespeople standing at your front door, peddling everything from vacuum cleaners to cell phones—none of which you are remotely interested in buying. Every few seconds, a new salesperson knocks on your door and won't stop until you open up. And when you do, he immediately launches into his pitch and won't take no for an answer.

What's the best way to get rid of this irritating intruder and not lose your cool or sanity in the process?

The best way is to open your door, look him in the eye, and firmly but politely say "No thank you." Then quickly close the door. By doing this, you remain disengaged and uninvolved with the situation, as opposed to losing your temper.

These pitchsters will never leave you alone, but you can still deal with them in a matter-of-fact way that doesn't cause you stress or upset—and can, in fact, be peaceful. This is what I call "Gracious Declining."

Remember this when you meditate this week: Your thoughts are like a never-ending line of salespeople, incessantly seeking your attention. You handle each of them in exactly the same way. Open the door, look them in the eye, and graciously decline to let them in.

Let's do it.

THIS WEEK'S MEDITATION INSTRUCTIONS:
GRACIOUS DECLINING

PREPARATION

- Start your timer for 8 minutes.

- Take your meditation position on your chair, comfortable and alert.

- Gently allow your eyes to close.

- Take a long, deep inhale that sweeps up your current worries, hopes, and dreams. Hold it for a moment. Then gently and slowly "sigh" it out.

- One more time. Deep breath. Release any remaining tension.

- Start your timer.

INSTRUCTIONS

- Allow your attention to rest lightly on your breath.

- A thought will shortly present itself in your awareness like an uninvited salesperson, knocking on your door.

- Be aware that the thought is here, demanding your attention.

- Firmly yet graciously, decline to engage the thought.

- Return attention to your breath. Sit quietly until another thought knocks on your door.

- Once more, graciously decline to engage this thought.

- Return to your breath again. Graciously decline whenever necessary.

- Do this until your timer sounds.

- Repeat this technique for 8 minutes a day for one week.

HOW'S IT GOING?

If you got a taste of Gracious Declining, you experienced how peaceful you can be when you refrain from engaging unwanted, frivolous, and negative thoughts.

Gracious Declining is not easy to do all the time. Your thoughts constantly try to convince you that what they are selling is crucial to your survival and you need to listen to them—*right now!* This is where a meditation practice like Gracious Declining—even for 8 minutes a day—can make an important difference. It allows you the space not to buy into the sales pitch.

You can also apply the Gracious Declining technique to body sensations. When a demanding body sensation appears in your doorway, treat it the same way you would an unwanted thought: Graciously decline to become involved with it.

Gracious Declining is a useful tool you can use every day. It's especially handy when dealing with tantrum-throwing children, telemarketers, and television commercials.

Q&A: PHYSICAL AND MENTAL INTRUSIONS

Q: Why Can't I Stop My Repetitive Thoughts?

I discussed this challenge in Week Three's Q&A in relation to song lyrics. Let's review it again in relation to repetitive thinking.

First you should know that you are not alone in the repetitive thought department. Everyone who meditates, from beginners to masters, experiences them somewhere along the line. I've been meditating for more than twenty-five years and still get ambushed by repetitive thoughts, although not nearly as much as I used to.

So what goes on here? Why does your mind seem to go into attack mode when you meditate, bombarding you with repetitive replays of fast-food jingles, old show tunes, and even worse, upsetting life experiences such as the fight you had with your boss this morning? It's as if there's a diabolical "instant replay" machine buried in your mind, and it's jammed, dooming you to watch the same scene over and over and over again.

Meditation can help you. You don't have to do anything special or learn any new technique. This is because the only difference between a random thought and a repetitive one is that the latter keeps recurring. All you need to do is treat it exactly the same way as you treat a single thought.

This means that when a thought that came and went and pops up again, you deal with it as if it's arising for the first time: Allow it, then release it. This is exactly in keeping with our Allow ... Allow ... Allow and Catch and Release Operating Instructions.

How many times must you do this? As long as the recurring thought recurs. But don't worry, it won't last forever. A repetitive thought, like any other thought, always moves on. All you need to do is relax, watch—and outlast it.

Q: *What If I Meditate and Feel Physical Pain?*

You stop meditation immediately!

It's not unusual to feel slight physical discomfort while meditating with your back unsupported. This should decrease as you continue your daily meditation practice. And remember what I said in the posture instructions: If you need to lean back on your chair for support, do so.

Chances are slim that sitting on a chair for 8 minutes will cause you to experience pain. But *if it ever does, immediately stop meditating and do whatever is necessary to remedy the situation.*

Q: I Really Need to Use the Restroom! Should I Stop Meditating?

The short answer to this question is: Go before you meditate. However, if the urge to go does arise, try the "I Have to Pee! Right Now! Meditation." Here's how:

Allow every thought, feeling, and body sensation surrounding the belief that you have to pee, *right this moment!* to arise and pass.

This meditation technique can be very useful, allowing you to see how your mind "amps up" what may only be slight physical discomfort. Also watch how your mind creates thoughts about your discomfort, such as feeling guilty for not peeing before you sat down. Or angry with a family member who made you too busy to pee. Or afraid you'll have "an accident."

Simply observe all of these thoughts, feelings, and body sensations as they arise and pass. Before you know it, your meditation timer will sound and you'll be done.

And also remember, as I've just said, if you experience real pain, *stop meditating immediately.*

*You're doing great! If this is your seventh day,
turn the page and move on to next week.*

WEEK SIX

PRIVATE SCREENING

WHERE YOU ARE

You're about to begin Week Six of your 8 Minute Meditation program. And by this point, you've got thirty-five meditation periods under your belt. Way to go!

If you've been following the program and meditating on a daily basis, you're probably at a point where:

• Meditation has become more effortless and part of your daily life.

• Your 8 minute meditation periods are taking you deeper into a place of peace and calm.

When things like this start to happen, it can mean that you're on the verge of experiencing your meditation "aha" moment. This is a deep, visceral, nonintellectual understanding—kind of a "cosmic click." It indicates that your meditation practice has shifted to a new level.

"Aha" moments are nothing mystical-shymistical; in fact, you've had plenty of them already in your life. Here's one:

Remember when you were a kid and learning to ride a bike for the first time? Mom or Dad fastened a set of training wheels on either side of your rear tire so you could experience "the feel" of riding a bike without tipping over.

Then came the big day: You were going to ride the bike all by yourself. Off came the training wheels. You mounted your bike and started to pedal. Mom and Dad ran alongside to steady you for a second. Then, suddenly, they released you!

And everything just clicked.

There you were, completely unsupported, riding your bike with complete balance. In that moment, when it all came together, something deep inside you, far beyond your thinking mind, nodded and *knew*.

Aha!

If you've already had this experience while you were in meditation, you understand what I'm talking about. If you haven't, don't worry; it doesn't mean that you're "meditation challenged." Just continue your daily 8 minute meditation periods without wondering if today's the "aha" day.

At some point, those training wheels will drop off—all by themselves.

WHAT YOU'LL BE DOING

This week you'll be working with a meditation technique called Private Screening. The anchor point for this meditation will be the virtual movie screen inside your head.

My friend, Josh Baran, entered a Zen monastery at the age of nineteen. After seven years as a monk, he returned to LA and opened a small public relations agency servicing nonprofit causes. Josh rapidly became one of the most sought-after PR people in the country, helping business and Hollywood celebrities, as well as the Dalai Lama.

Josh recommends the Private Screening technique to people who he helps learn to meditate. He likes it because it involves something everyone has already mastered—watching a computer, TV, or movie screen.

Private Screening also lends itself quite nicely to 8 Minute Meditation: your 8 minute meditation periods are the same length as the space between two commercial breaks of a TV show. This makes meditation like watching your favorite program—the one written, directed, and starring you.

To get a taste of Private Screening, try this mini-meditation:

• Take a deep breath and gently allow your eyes to close.

• Allow any and all visual images to arise without resisting them.

• Notice if there is a place inside your head upon which these images seem to be projected.

- Do this for about two minutes.

- Open your eyes.

When you did this mini-meditation, did you observe that your visual images seem to be projected onto a kind of "projection screen" located just behind your eyes? In Private Screening, this "mind screen" will serve as your anchor point, the place where you gently yet alertly rest awareness during your meditation period. From this place, you'll observe the visual images projected on your screen. When thoughts arise, you'll do what you always do in meditation: Realize they are there and return attention to your anchor point.

Remember, the operative word in Private Screening is *observe*. All you need to do is observe your screen. There is no need to make sense of this movie. Leave that to those geniuses out in Hollywood.

This would be a good time to remind you of two pertinent operating instructions as they apply to Private Screening:

- **Allow . . . allow . . . allow.** In meditation, everything is included—and nothing is excluded. There's no need to wonder why an image of beef lo mein just popped up. It just did. Just allow it.

- **Catch and release.** As soon as you realize that you've "hooked" a visual image, that's your cue to drop it. Regard Private Screening as you would a nonstop slide show. A slide appears, stays on screen for a second or two, and then is replaced by another. And another.

Private Screening offers you a beautiful opportunity to observe your own myriad, nonstop mental images. While your eyes may be closed, this week will be a real eye-opener.

Let's begin.

THIS WEEK'S MEDITATION INSTRUCTIONS:
PRIVATE SCREENING

PREPARATION

- Set your timer for 8 minutes.

- Take your meditation position on your chair, comfortable and alert.

- Gently allow your eyes to close.

- Take a long, deep inhale that sweeps up your current worries, hopes, and dreams. Hold it for a moment. Then gently and slowly "sigh" it out.

- One more time. Deep breath. Release any remaining tension.

- Start your timer.

INSTRUCTIONS

- Bring your attention to your "inner projection screen" located just behind your eyes. This will be your anchor point.

- An image will appear on the screen. It can be a picture of anything, projected in many ways: fuzzy, distinct, black and white, wildly colorful.

- Just observe this image without judgment, analysis, or questioning.

- Let this image do its dance. It may intensify. It may suddenly disappear. It could dissolve into a new image. Allow it to do whatever it wants.

- Just watch this play of images. Allow them to come and go. Do not make up stories about them. You are just the watcher, not the writer, actor, or director of this movie.

- Caught up in thinking? Good. Notice this. Release the thought, without the slightest self-judgment. Return attention to your anchor point, your inner projection screen.

- Do this until your timer sounds.

- Repeat this technique for 8 minutes a day for one week.

HOW'S IT GOING?

You probably didn't have to wait very long for a visual image to appear on your projection screen. You closed your eyes and— *voilà!*—there it was. And your mind probably immediately leapt in, doing its job to concoct some logical, cohesive story about what you saw. Private Screening Meditation is designed to help you become more aware of this lock-step habit—and help you break it. Here's what I mean:

When you neutrally observe what arises on your private projection screen, the compulsion to do something about it diminishes. This lets you settle more deeply into peace and calm, allowing you to see how few of your thoughts merit the vital importance you place on them.

Newton Minow, former chairman of the Federal Communications Commission, once referred to television as "the vast wasteland." The same is true of the programming that appears on the TV screen in your mind. This is one of the great gifts of meditation: It allows you to eradicate this clutter and create space for what truly is important.

Q&A: DOUBTS AND FEARS

Q: I Should Be Farther Along in Meditation by Now. After All, It's Been More Than Five Weeks!

Five weeks . . . that long, huh?

It's completely understandable to want to see a sign that your hard work is paying off, that you've gotten somewhere. But as I said, wa-a-a-y back in Part I, meditation is an ongoing process, not a goal. There is really no place you need to arrive.

But this doesn't mean that you can't move forward. You can. Here are a few examples of what I mean by progress:

• A feeling of being both more alert, yet calmer. This goes hand in hand with a sense of being more present in the moment—here, as opposed to elsewhere or elsewhen.

• A sense of being more emotionally stable and less swept away by the highs and lows of life's roller coaster, even in the face of serious life challenges.

• The deepening ability to neutrally observe the rising and passing of thoughts, images, and sensations during meditation.

Here's another thing you can do to see how far you've come in the past six weeks. Try my Meditation Progress Check. Take a few minutes, close your eyes, and, without any pressure on yourself, ponder this question:

How do I feel today as opposed to how I felt six weeks ago?

Okay. What came up for you? Perhaps you zeroed in on some of the progress markers I've just described. Maybe different ones. But one thing I hope you realized is this: *You are more aware and present today than you were six weeks ago.*

This in and of itself is tremendous progress.

Q: I Suddenly Burst into Tears While I Was Meditating. It Upset Me.

Don't be upset. It's completely natural for intense feelings and emotions to arise both during and after a meditation period.

Meditation allows us to "let off steam"—in the best, most positive, and least destructive way possible. Here's an analogy to help you understand what I mean:

Imagine you are a tightly sealed, bubbling cauldron, with steam rising from your very depths. This "steam" is composed of your buried, deep-seated emotional feelings and thoughts. It makes no difference what they are or how they got there.

Now, let's add meditation to this scenario. Imagine meditation as a kind of catalyst, raising the internal temperature of the cauldron to critical mass, until the lid can no longer withstand the pressure, and as they used to say at sea, "Thar she blows!"

As your cauldron lid flies off into space, billows of emotional steam instantly escape, releasing those unconscious and suppressed feelings and thoughts.

How do you cope with the emotional volcanoes that arise during meditation? *In exactly the same way you deal with anything and everything else that arises in meditation.* You allow . . . allow . . . allow. You catch and release. You take a deep breath—and return to your meditation technique. In sum, you do whatever works for you in that moment.

The release of deep emotions during meditation offers you a superb opportunity to put into practice what you've learned over the past weeks. Don't take to the hills. Take advantage.

Q: I'm Afraid Meditation Will Make Me Too "Laid Back" and That I'll Lose My "Edge" at Work, School, and Sports.

A simple, daily meditation practice won't dull your competitive edge. On the contrary, it will hone it.

Mention the word *meditation,* and people envision shaved-headed monks, lolling about at some remote monastery, doing nothing, and—of course—going nowhere. This, by the way, is far from accurate. Monks work as hard as the rest of us do.

Nevertheless, this connotation of meditation with indolence does not inspire confidence among those of us who may be pulling an all-nighter to get that appeal brief filed, going the extra mile to train for the Boston Marathon, or preparing for the SAT.

In fact, the truth is just the opposite: The practice of meditation doesn't dull your edge—it sharpens it. As you know, I began to meditate in my second year of law school, which is not exactly an environment known for encouraging laziness and sloth. I followed that up with more than ten years as a lawyer, producer, and writer in the entertainment business, where getting a "green light" on a project is the equivalent of turning a Carnival cruise ship around with a sailboat.

Throughout all of this, meditation played a vital role in my success. It worked for me and it can work for you. Why? Because the consistent, daily practice of meditation sets the stage for the unerring and natural intelligence within you to effortlessly emerge. This is the intuitive wisdom that knows exactly what you need to do and the best and most effective way to do it. That means that you find yourself effortlessly acting in a more appropriate, efficient, and productive way.

So don't be afraid. Meditation won't hold you back. It will help you move ahead.

You're doing great! If this is your seventh day,
turn the page and move on to next week.

LOVINGKINDNESS MEDITATION ⏱

WHERE YOU ARE

Congratulations! You've reached Week Seven. You're rounding the far turn and heading down the home stretch of your 8 Minute Meditation program.

At this point you have incorporated meditation practice into your life. It's become part of your daily routine, like taking your morning shower or brushing your teeth. This is a sure sign of your growing understanding that meditation is not some big mystical-shmystical deal. It's more like a walk in the park than a visit to Swami Watchamacallit's Kingdom of Bliss.

At this point, you're a real meditator with a deepening meditation practice. You've reached the point where you regard meditation not as something you *have* to do, but something you *want and need* to do. You know it's changing your life—for the better.

You've made great strides with meditation the past six weeks, and you deserve a major hug and pat on the back. And that's exactly what you're going to get: This week I'm introducing you to a different, special kind of meditation. It's called Lovingkindness Meditation. And this one especially "tastes good. And is good for you, too!"

Let's carry on.

WHAT YOU'LL BE DOING

Up until this week, 8 Minute Meditation has focussed on developing Mindfulness Muscle using concentration and awareness techniques. During this period, you've hopefully established a new, more accepting relationship with your thoughts, feelings, and emotions.

This week, you're going to learn a technique that can nurture a richer and more accepting relationship between you and your heart. It is called Lovingkindness Meditation and, quite simply, it is about sending your best wishes to the entire world—starting with *you*. Just like charity, Lovingkindness Meditation begins at home.

Let me ask you a question: When was the last time you wished yourself love and kindness, for no reason other than that you're completely entitled to it?

Probably not too recently, right?

All of us, to varying degrees, have difficulty being kind to ourselves. It's one of life's ironies that we can always find the heart and compassion to forgive someone who's wronged us. But just you do the same thing, and brother!—you never hear the end of it from your severest critic—*you*!

It's clear that each of us can use some help in the self-kindness department. Lovingkindness Meditation can be a powerful ally in this regard. The practice of lovingkindness complements the practice of concentration, helping to integrate both aspects into a more complete meditation practice. Here's one way to look at it:

We all know that a bird needs two strong wings to fly straight and true. So does your meditation practice. By now, you've developed the wing of awareness and concentration. Now it's time to build the other wing: lovingkindness. When you can flap both these wings strongly, your meditation practice can really soar.

The *8 Minute Meditation* version of Lovingkindness Meditation is easy, straightforward, simple, and pleasant to do. But before we begin, here's a word on sitting posture for Lovingkindness Meditation. There is only one requirement and that is that you be comfortable. You can even lie down if you like—without of course, taking a "meditation snooze." And if that should happen, for goodness sake, don't berate yourself. Just sit up and start Lovingkindness Meditation again.

There's nothing forced, mystical-shmystical, or phony about doing Lovingkindness Meditation. It's an expression of your true nature. As the Buddha once said, you can search the entire world for someone who is worthier of kindness than yourself—and you will never find him or her.

With this truth in mind, turn the page and let's begin.

THIS WEEK'S MEDITATION INSTRUCTIONS:
LOVINGKINDNESS

PREPARATION

- Set your timer for 8 minutes.

- Take your meditation position on your chair, comfortable and alert.

- Gently allow your eyes to close.

- Take a long, deep inhale that sweeps up your current worries, hopes, and dreams. Hold it for a moment. Then gently and slowly "sigh" it out.

- One more time. Deep breath. Release any remaining tension.

- Start your timer.

INSTRUCTIONS

- Recall any act of kindness you ever did. This can be something very major or very minor, even holding a door open for someone.

- Allow yourself to feel how you felt when you performed that act. Notice sensations of warmth and flow, particularly in your chest and heart areas. Relax and *really* allow yourself to feel this.

- With your body steeping in this feeling, silently say the following phrases:

  May I be happy.

  May I have ease of being.

- Relax. Allow each phrase to rise from deep down in your heart. Let it mingle with your felt sense of kindness. Let go into this.

- Repeat the phrases again: **May I be happy. May I have ease of being.** Allow your entire being to express them.

- Now, repeat the two phrases, substituting "all beings" for "I":

  May all beings be happy.

  May all beings have ease of being.

- Relax. Allow the phrases to resonate and melt into your felt sense of kindness.

- Repeat again: **May I be happy. May I have ease of being.**

- Alternate these two sets of phrases until your timer sounds.

- Repeat this technique for 8 minutes a day for one week.

HOW'S IT GOING?

You may be surprised that you experienced difficulty and resistance with Lovingkindness Meditation. Don't feel bad; you're not alone.

On an intellectual level, the idea of sending yourself your kindest wishes and thoughts sounds easy. But the actual act of sending yourself the same best wishes you would send to someone else can be quite challenging. It's amazing how something so simple can be so complicated by personal beliefs about sincerity, selfishness, and ego.

If you encountered a challenge with lovingkindness, here's my suggestion: Practice it lightly with self-forgiveness and take the long view. Here's what I mean:

Imagine it's a beautiful October afternoon, and you're out planting tulip bulbs in your garden. What's your expectation of them? That they will mature and pop up as fully grown flowers by this time tomorrow? Of course not; you realize that the growth and blossoming of a flower requires time, a nourishing and nurturing environment, and patience.

When you engage in Lovingkindness Meditation, you also plant seeds—of lovingkindness. It may take some time before they blossom. But just as a tulip bulb knows exactly how to grow and when to open, so does your heart. All you need to do is tend your garden, relax—and trust.

You might not see the fruits of Lovingkindness Meditation today, but I promise you have already sown seeds that will blossom.

Q&A: LOVINGKINDNESS

Q: I Love Lovingkindness Meditation! Can I Do It for More Than 8 Minutes? Or After My Regular Meditation?

Absolutely.

If you enjoy Lovingkindness Meditation, I encourage you to expand and deepen your practice. You can, whenever you like, go to Part III of this book, where you'll find more material on lovingkindness, including a set of expanded Lovingkindness Meditation instructions and more Q&As.

There are also several books on the market whose subject is the practice of Lovingkindness Meditation. I recommend these:

• *Lovingkindness: The Revolutionary Art of Happiness* by Sharon Salzberg (Shambala). This is the "primer" for anyone interested in Lovingkindness Meditation, written by one of our foremost teachers and practitioners. Sharon's talks and guided meditation tapes are also available through the Dharma Seed Tape Library.

• *Radical Acceptance: Embracing Your Life with the Heart of a Buddha* by Tara Brach (Bantam). Tara is both a therapist and meditation teacher. Her book offers excellent insights into Lovingkindness Meditation, particularly the obstacles one encounters due to what Tara calls "the trance of unworthiness." You can buy it as a book or on tape from Sounds True under the title *Radical Self-Acceptance*.

• *The Art of Forgiveness, Lovingkindness, and Peace* by Jack Kornfield (Bantam). Jack is one of America's distinguished Insight Meditation teachers as well as a founder of Spirit Rock Meditation Center. His message is clear and compassionate: No matter where you are, peace and kindness are only a breath away.

You'll find information on how to order the tape versions of Sharon's and Tara's books in Part III.

One thing though—before you start adding more Lovingkindness Meditation to your meditation practice, it's important that you examine your motivation for doing so. Should you discover that your zeal lies in the belief that "If I just do this long enough, I'll really *feel* lovingkindness toward others and myself"— that's not a good reason to increase lovingkindness practice. Here's why:

By now, you know that trying to attain any kind of state is antithetical to what 8 Minute Meditation is all about. In fact, it's practically a guarantee that you will never experience what you're trying so hard to experience. So please, conduct your own internal inquiry and see what comes up.

If Lovingkindness Meditation makes you even a little happier, I'm happy. It's a great daily meditation practice to do, not just for others but for yourself.

Now, let's do something amazing, something you thought impossible just seven short weeks ago . . . move on to the last and (tada!) final week of your 8 Minute Meditation program.

COMBINATION PLATE

WHERE YOU ARE

Congratulations! You have reached the eighth and final week of the 8 Minute Meditation program.

Do the math, and you'll find that you've now meditated for 392 minutes! That's more than six and a half hours! This is equivalent to watching *The Matrix Trilogy* or six episodes of *Law and Order*. And trust me, you've spent your time much more wisely.

In this, your last week of the 8 Minute Meditation program, don't be surprised if you still feel that:

- You don't understand what meditation is.

- You should be farther along in meditation.

- Meditation should be easier at this point and it isn't.

- You should be a "better meditator."

- You are a failure and meditation is not for you.

On the other end of the spectrum you might believe that, in just seven weeks, you've totally mastered meditation. Been there, done that, got the T-shirt, and now you don't have to meditate ever again.

As you know by now, and as I said at the beginning of the program, meditation is not too easy—and not too hard. There's no way you can be a failure—or a master. But what is true is this: Over the past seven weeks, you have laid the foundation for a strong meditation practice that will continue to grow—and can last your lifetime.

Let's conduct a quick reality check on where you are right now with your meditation practice:

- Gently close your eyes.

- Take a deep breath and settle down.

- Allow your mind to review the events of the past few days.

- Find one incident, event, or experience that you found yourself reacting to differently than you normally would. This does not have to be a big thing. It can be as small as how you took a sip of tea.

- In that moment, how did you feel? More peaceful, relaxed, less tense? More aware, alert, accepting? More present in the moment, more alive?

- Open your eyes.

If you have been meditating on a daily basis for the past seven weeks, you probably recalled at least one such moment. Maybe it was on Tuesday, when you were stuck in that endless line at the bank, yet found yourself calmer than usual, perhaps noticing how you had naturally dropped into watching your breath. Perhaps the moment occurred last night, when you washed the dinner dishes and found yourself really feeling how pleasant the warm, sudsy water felt on your wrists.

Although these might seem like minor things, the truth is that they are significant. What's happening is the transformation of the ordinary into the extraordinary: You're waking up and seeing the world fresh and new.

This is the power of meditation. And now that you've got it, let's move on to Week Eight.

WHAT YOU'LL BE DOING

Combination Plate technique is the most subtle and advanced technique in the 8 Minute Meditation program. It's a tad more complicated than choosing one item from column A and one from column B, but don't worry or feel intimidated; Combination Plate is merely an amalgam of several of the 8 minute meditation techniques you've already spent weeks practicing.

In Week Two of the program, you worked with Naked Sound Meditation, where you listened to sounds without interpreting them. Then, in Week Three, Noting Body Sensations, you observed the physical arisings in your body. More recently, in Week Six, Private Screening, you observed the visual images that appeared on the projection screen behind your eyes. Now, you're going to use these three techniques in concert.

Combination Plate is a little like learning to juggle. Here's the overview:

- A thought, body sensation, or visual image arises.

- You allow it, observe it, and label it as one of the following three things:

  - Talk
  - Body sensation
  - Image

- Another phenomenon arises. You do the same thing.

- If a new event arises while one is already in your awareness, make room for it and label it as well. For example, you might be observing your breath when a visual image of driving your car arises. Your labeling would thus be: "body . . . body . . . image . . . image and body . . . image and body."

Here's a sample of what a few seconds of labeling might be like:

Image . . . image . . . body . . . body and image . . . image . . . talk . . . talk . . . talk and image . . . talk and image and body . . . image . . . talk . . . image.

Don't become upset when you find yourself left behind in the dust of fast-moving phenomena. It happens to everyone. And it's not important. What is important is the quality of attention you bring to observing whatever does come up. When you find yourself left behind, treat it as though you've just missed a bus. Another will be along shortly. All you need to do is relax, wait for it to pull up, and hop on.

Combination Plate Meditation can have a very powerful effect: It can keep you so busy observing rising and subsiding phenomena that you, in a way, "lose track" of yourself. And when the sense of "you" drops away, you can experience a deep sense of awareness called the "witness state."

Remember back to the earlier *Dragnet* quote? You might say that the witness state is "Just the facts, ma'am"—written large. The witness state can feel unsettling, blissful, and anything in between. Just allow whatever it is to be whatever it is. Neither hold on to nor run from it. As you know, everything, including the witness state, comes and goes, like clouds scudding across the open sky.

So relax and do your best. As our operating instruction says, "Have fun with it!"

THIS WEEK'S MEDITATION INSTRUCTIONS:
COMBINATION PLATE

PREPARATION

- Set your timer for 8 minutes.

- Take your meditation position on your chair, comfortable and alert.

- Gently allow your eyes to close.

- Take a long, deep inhale that sweeps up your current worries, hopes, and dreams. Hold it for a moment. Then gently and slowly "sigh" it out.

- One more time. Deep breath. Release any remaining tension.

- Start your timer.

INSTRUCTIONS

- Something arises in your awareness.

- Note this phenomenon as one of the following:

  - Talk, inside or outside your mind
  - Body sensation
  - Visual image

- Label the phenomenon using *one* of these words:

  - Talk
  - Body
  - Image

- Observe the rise and fall of this phenomenon.

- Another phenomenon arises. Expand your awareness to include it. Label it as talk, body, or image.

- When more than one experience simultaneously occupies your awareness, note each as best you can. They may rise and fall together or in counterpoint.

- If you fall behind in your labeling, you need not try to catch up. Just stop where you are, take a deep breath, and wait for the next phenomenon to present itself.

- Don't feel frustrated if you cannot follow everything perfectly. Just neutrally observe: talk, body, or image, singly, in tandem, or all at once. Allow everything to rise and fade away.

- Do this until your timer sounds.

- Repeat this technique for 8 minutes a day for one week.

HOW'S IT GOING?

Combination Plate is a challenging meditation technique. That's why I saved it for last. Consider it your "final exam," which you've now passed with flying colors!

Although you might have experienced some confusion, irritation, and frustration while doing Combination Plate, don't regard it as an indication of how far you need to go, *but how far you've come.* If I had given you Combination Plate in Week One, you probably would have thrown up your hands—and thrown away this book!

Instead, here you are in just eight weeks, able to comprehend and perform a meditation technique that requires a high level of allowance, awareness, and concentration. Congratulations! You are a meditator, with a meditation practice that can last you a lifetime, and one that I hope you will take to the next level, which is what Part III of this book is all about.

For those of you who have diligently followed this 8 week program, meditation is obviously something that resonates deeply within you. And I'll bet you are raring to get on to Part III. The following advice is directed to anybody who, for any reason, may have worked with the 8 Minute Meditation program sporadically or is reading these words because they thought they could skip the previous hundred pages and just "cut to the chase."

If you fall into either category, please do not berate yourself or think you are a failure or "meditation challenged." If you only meditated once in the past 8 weeks, this is one more time than you have ever meditated before. And here's how simple and easy it is to start to meditate again: *Return to where you last were in the program and start from there.*

As I've said many times, there is no such thing as success or failure in meditation. This is a *practice,* not something you do once, for 8 days or even 8 weeks and then cross off your "to do" list. Meditation is an ongoing process, a journey in awareness, clarity, and happiness. Not in some abstract future—but now, *right in this moment.*

Whether you've meditated for the past 8 weeks with ease or consider yourself a total failure, my advice is the same: Keep meditating. Every day. For at least 8 minutes.

Q&A: GRADUATION QUESTIONS

Q: *Eight Weeks of Meditation, and I Still Can't Stop Thinking. What's Wrong?*

Nothing is wrong, except your belief that something's wrong.

The notion that meditation will, at some point, cause the complete cessation of thinking is what I call "The Great Meditation Misconception." It's a misbelief held by almost every beginning meditator—and plenty of advanced ones too. Allow me to say this again: *There is no way you will ever stop your mind from thinking.* That is its job: to think, analyze, criticize, and judge—365/24/7.

You have already heard me say that in 8 Minute Meditation, our goal is not to suppress thinking but *surpass* it. The following scenario illustrates what I mean:

Imagine you have a fruitcake relative. Let's call her Aunt Fran. She's not dangerous, just obsessed with UFOs, which she believes are about to make a guest appearance at your local Wal-Mart. And that's exactly where you and Aunt Fran are this very moment, shopping for a toaster oven.

So there you are, in the small appliance aisle, trying to figure out what the best buy is, while Aunt Fran incessantly chatters in your ear about the imminent UFO invasion.

Nerve-racking? Absolutely. The question is, how do you handle this situation the best way for all concerned—including Aunt Fran?

You could rush over and tell the store manager to start the UFO Preparedness Drill. Or scream at dear, little old Aunt Fran to shut up. You could perhaps tow her out to the parking lot and lock her in the car with your Schnauzer.

But are you going to do that? Of course not! Because you are sane, kind—and darn it—you need a toaster oven! So what do you do?

Absolutely nothing.

Right. You just allow Aunt Fran to chatter away about those aliens. Every minute or so, you automatically nod your head, smile, and say "Uh-huh" or "Right." *In other words, you hear the chatter and pay no attention to it.* Your focus is on those toaster ovens. Aunt Fran's words are just "white noise."

Let's apply this scenario to thoughts and meditation. Think of Aunt Fran as none other than good old Roving Mind, the nonstop, chattering voice that constantly wants to engage you in ridiculous, useless, and unhelpful thinking. Imagine the toaster oven as a meditation anchor point, like your breath.

What you're doing when you meditate is exactly what you're doing in the Wal-Mart: allowing Aunt Fran/Roving Mind to chatter away, while you keep your attention on the toaster oven/anchor point.

So don't worry, you didn't miss the secret thought-stopping technique I cleverly hid on page 48. Roving Mind is here to stay. Regard it as a gift that's here to remind you that peace is just around the corner, when you allow thoughts to come and go their merry—and sometimes wacky—way.

Q: Can Meditation Help Me Eat More Healthfully? Or Lose Weight?

It could—if you meditate on a StairMaster.

Even though 8 Minute Meditation is a kind of diet for your

mind, you're not going to lose a lot of weight sitting on a chair for 8 minutes a day.

There is, however, something else in your question we can explore: Can meditation make you wiser in your choice of diet? My answer to that question is yes; it is certainly possible, after you've been meditating for some time, to find yourself making healthier, more positive choices in and changes to your diet and lifestyle.

For example, you could, one day and for no apparent reason, find yourself cutting back on your five triple-latte-espresso habit, first to three cups, then one—eventually maybe none! This change might not seem to be a result of a conscious decision, but rather something that "just happened."

But what might really be happening here is that meditation is making you more aware of your unconscious and automatic behavior, in this case one that may be unhealthy. This seemingly effortless lifestyle change is yet another example of how meditation, rather than depriving you of things you like, provides you a mindful opportunity to notice that something might not be good for you. And take action.

Q: Even After 8 Weeks of Meditation, I Still Feel Strange When I Do It.

As I've said, it's natural to feel awkward about the process of meditation, especially in the early stages of practice. It's also normal to feel that you're doing something "countercultural" when you meditate. After all, your decision to devote even 8 minutes a day of your busy life to something that may not be considered "productive" in the eyes of the world can make you feel ashamed, embarrassed, and maybe even guilty.

Here's a way of looking at meditation that can help you accept these feelings of awkwardness and strangeness: Treat your meditation practice in the same way you would a new romantic relationship. Here's what I mean:

The first few weeks of a budding relationship are what's known as the "getting-to-know-you" or "honeymoon" phase. Everything is fresh and new, and you are excited about the possibilities. But at the same time, you feel some trepidation, hesitancy, and even anxiety about what you may have gotten yourself into.

However, because you really care for this person, you decide to "give it a chance" and see what develops. Eventually, as in every romance, you reach the point where it becomes clear as to whether things are going to work out or not.

It's the same with meditation: It seems new and strange at first, but part of that feeling may be due to the excitement of discovering something that has great potential for your happiness.

Stick around and give it a chance. Trust me, it will work out.

CONGRATULATIONS!! AND A PREVIEW OF COMING ATTRACTIONS

You made it! Way to go!

Eight weeks ago, you probably thought you would never be able to meditate on a daily basis for 8 seconds, much less 8 weeks. But you did! And now here you are, with a strong meditation practice that can last you a lifetime.

I'm not saying that it was smooth sailing all the way. That's not the way meditation—or life—goes. Whether you've been meditating for twenty minutes, twenty days, or twenty years, some days feel like a cakewalk, while others feel like a *schlep* over the Himalayas.

You've done well! Rest on your laurels for a few minutes. And then, move on to Part III of 8 Minute Meditation. I call it the "upgrade" section, and it is designed to help you take your meditation practice to the next level.

Part III also contains additional Lovingkindness Meditation instructions, my personal "A-list" of books and tapes, and lots of other goodies. Perhaps most important, Part III will introduce and teach you what I call the Meditation in Action Template, a simple yet powerful technique that enables you to apply Mindfulness Muscle to any daily activity—and transform it into a different, richer experience. Be sure you try it; you'll be glad you did.

Just before you move on, you need to do one more thing. It's time to exchange the *8 Minute Meditation* pledge that you signed 8 weeks ago for your well-earned *8 Minute Meditation* Certificate of Completion!

8 MINUTE MEDITATION
Official Certificate of Completion
With Honors

(Date) _____

Be it known to all concerned, that (your name) _____
has successfully completed the 8 Minute Meditation program
with flying colors.

In accordance with completion, the recipient is now
declared a meditator, equipped with the basic skills needed to
deepen their meditation practice and continue it for their lifetime.

Furthermore, they are entitled to all the benefits of meditation, including the ability to be more present, allow what is,
and in general, lead a fuller, happier life.

Victor N. Davich
8 Minute Meditation

AND REMEMBER . . .

The fact that you have given yourself a meditation practice is a
sure sign that you desire more peace and happiness in your life—
and the lives of others. Continue to make it so.

As I have said throughout these past 8 weeks, remember to
treat yourself with great kindness in everything you do, including
your meditation practice.

It has been a privilege to spend the last 8 weeks with you.

PART III

• • •

THE UPGRADE

WELCOME TO THE *8 MINUTE MEDITATION* UPGRADE

From soft drinks to computer software, you can't go through a day without someone offering you an upgrade. So why should *8 Minute Meditation* be different! ?

First of all, I want you to know that there's no catch to your upgrade: It's *absolutely, totally, positively free!* You got it just by buying the book. And even better news: You're absolutely ready to upgrade your meditation practice. In fact, you'll be doing yourself a great service by doing so.

"WHAT'S IN IT FOR ME TO UPGRADE?"

The ultimate goal of *8 Minute Meditation* is to empower you with a way of being—not for just 8 minutes a day sitting on a chair, but the millions of other minutes that comprise your life.

8 Minute Meditation has thus far helped you give yourself a consistent, daily 8 minute meditation practice. But why stop here? The truth is that meditation has incredible *practical value* that can be applied to everything you do. Honestly, if you confine meditation to 8 minutes a day sitting on a chair, not only are you missing the point of meditation, but you're shortchanging yourself as well.

Your initial response to what I've just said could very well be, *Are you crazy? If I float around all day in a meditative state, I won't be able to function!* But the truth is just the opposite. Let's take a closer look at what you perceive as your ordinary state and see just how awake you really are.

Right now, I'd like you to take a minute or so and review the myriad chores and activities you performed today. Choose one of them. Now look closely at it and answer this question:

Were you truly there when you did it? Or were you on some kind of "automatic pilot"?

For example take eating your breakfast. Did you eat your eggs and really taste them? Or were you simultaneously listening to the morning news, scanning your e-mail, preparing lunch for your son, and chatting on the phone with your friend?

Choose some more activities. No matter which ones you select, I'm pretty sure that you'll find they share one thing in common: You really weren't completely "there" when you did them. Pretty amazing, huh? Maybe a little scary, too.

Now, look at one activity and consider how effectively you performed it while you were on automatic pilot. Is it possible that you could have done it more effortlessly, thoroughly, productively, and happily if you had actually been *here,* as opposed to elsewhere or elsewhen? The answer is obvious.

Well, here's good news. The goal of the 8 Minute Meditation is to help you do exactly that. Part III affords you the opportunity to take what you have learned in the past 8 weeks to the next level, so you can be more present—more *here*—right now. Not just sitting on a chair for 8 minutes a day, but everywhere you are.

What's in it for you to go deeper in meditation? A richer experience of life. Interested? Sure you are.

CARRYING ON WITH MEDITATION. CARRYING MEDITATION INTO LIFE.

Part III is designed to help you deepen your meditation practice and apply it to daily life. It is divided into four sections:

- **Beyond 8 Minutes** enables you to effortlessly and effectively increase your daily meditation time. It will assist you in creating your own meditation "training schedule" as well as your personal "mini-retreat."

- **Meditation in Action** will enable you to carry over your meditation practice into daily life. You'll learn about and use the Meditation in Action Template, a simple yet powerful tool you can apply to any activity in your day. It also enables you to build Mindfulness Muscle. Once you see how easy and effective the template is, you'll want to use it all the time.

• **Lovingkindness: Going Further** will help you deepen your connection with the world, in the world.

• **Resources** is my personal "A-list" of books, tapes, and retreat centers that can help you take your meditation practice to the next level. The section also will inform you about meditation sitting groups and how to find one, or start one of your own.

You've sat down long enough in meditation. Now it's time for you to stand up and take it into every part of your daily life.
Let's start to upgrade.

BEYOND 8 MINUTES

The two simplest and easiest ways to increase your meditation time are:

• The gradual addition of minutes to your current 8 minute meditation period.

• The addition of a daily second meditation period.

You may utilize these options alone or in tandem. I'll show you how. But first, you'll need to select your favorite meditation technique from the last 8 weeks of the 8 Minute Meditation program. The technique you choose will be the one you stay with as you begin to increase your meditation time.

How to Choose Your Technique

Over the past 8 weeks, you've learned and practiced meditation with 8 different meditation techniques. Different techniques resonate more deeply for certain people. It's quite probable that you've already decided on a favorite. If you have, you can skip to the next section. If you haven't, please do the following:

- Return to Part II and review the 8 meditation techniques you've worked with, excluding Lovingkindness Meditation.

- Close your eyes and spend a minute with each of them. You'll probably find one or more that you "connect with."

- Now, narrow your choice down to one technique. Got it? Great. This is the meditation technique you will use exclusively as you increase your meditation time.

How to Increase Your Time Period

The easiest way to increase meditation time is to incrementally add minutes to your daily 8 minute period. This is analogous to how you would train for a walkathon or marathon, gradually and slowly, so as not to cause yourself unnecessary strain or pressure.

Begin by adding two minutes a day to your current 8 minute session. Meditate for this ten-minute period for two weeks. Then, add another two minutes of meditation, making it twelve. Here's what this "training schedule" looks like:

- **Weeks 1 and 2:** 10 minutes

- **Weeks 3 and 4:** 12 minutes

- **Weeks 5 and 6:** 14 minutes

- **Weeks 7 and 8:** 16 minutes

- **Weeks 9 and 10:** 18 minutes

The gradual addition of two minutes every two weeks may seem insignificant, but remember what Einstein said about compound interest: Things add up. Start today, and by the end of about two months, you will be meditating for eighteen minutes a day! This is a serious meditation practice by anyone's standards.

After you've gotten your meditation time where you want it, continue at this level, using your chosen meditation technique for a minimum of two more weeks. At that point, if you like, you can switch techniques.

But remember, once you choose your technique, there's got to be no "buyer's remorse" or second-guessing—no matter what. Stick with the meditation technique you chose. Just as there is no such thing as a "bad" or "wrong" meditation period, there is no such thing as a wrong meditation technique.

How to Add a Second Daily Meditation Period

The next option for deepening your meditation practice is to add a second daily 8 minute meditation period. The addition of a second 8 minute meditation period immediately doubles your meditation time to sixteen minutes a day. This may sound overwhelming, but the fact that it's divided into two equal portions makes it easy and doable.

People who meditate usually do it twice a day, first thing in the morning and last thing before bed. I recommend this. Should you decide on other times of the day, allow at least six hours between meditation periods.

You may also increase your second meditation period in increments, as described in the previous section. For example:

- **Weeks 1 and 2:** morning period, 8 minutes; evening period, 2 minutes

- **Weeks 3 and 4:** morning period, 8 minutes; evening period, 4 minutes

And so on.

If you do it like this, you will eventually reach the point where you are meditating for twenty minutes, twice a day, for a total of forty minutes! This is a major meditation practice, one that will lead you to more advanced levels of practice. In fact, if you do reach this point in your practice, give some serious consideration to going on a meditation retreat. You'll find pointers on how to locate one in the next section.

And remember, there are no hard-and-fast rules here. Feel free to experiment. Mix and match. When you find something that "feels right," stay with it. You'll know when it's time for more minutes.

The Personal Mini-Retreat: Spending Quality Time with Meditation

Personal mini-retreats are a great way to deepen your practice. And you don't need to travel to a retreat center or monastery. All you need are a few undisturbed hours at home.

If you went to a retreat at a meditation center, you might spend many hours each day alternating between sitting and walking meditation periods. On your mini-retreat, you will meditate and walk, but for shorter periods and many fewer hours.

Here's how to plan and conduct your mini-retreat:

• Reserve at least one hour when you can be alone and undisturbed by work, family, or other responsibilities.

• Create a space that is as quiet and intrusion-free as possible. Turn off the phone. Close the doors. Hang a sign on the door that says "On Retreat. Back at 4."

• Prepare a short, simple schedule, alternating amounts of time for sitting meditation and walking meditation (using the Meditation in Action Template in the next section). In the beginning, keep time periods short.

• Settle down and follow your schedule.

Here's a sample schedule for a two-hour mini-retreat:

12:45–1:00 Prepare space and quiet down.

1:00–1:15 Sit.

1:15–1:30 Walk (using the Meditation in Action Template).

1:30–1:45 Sit.

1:45–2:00 Meditation in Action: Just one Dish Meditation.

2:00–2:30 Listen to meditation teaching tape.

2:15–2:30 Walk.

2:30–2:45 Sit.

2:45–3:00 Lovingkindness Meditation.

As you can see, you can fit a lot of meditation into just two hours. The mini-retreat is also a great opportunity for you to push your personal meditation "envelope" (with kindness, of course!). For instance, you might decide that you're going to sit for twelve minute periods even though your daily practice is only at 8.

Teaching and guided meditation tapes can contribute greatly to the quality of your mini-retreat. That's why I've set aside time for you to listen to them. When you do, give them the same, undivided attention as you would your meditation periods. You will find some good resources for tapes later on in this section.

THE MEDITATION IN ACTION TEMPLATE

The Meditation in Action Template is a terrific tool that lets you take the awareness and presence you develop in sitting meditation and apply it to all your daily activities, no matter how simple or complicated they are. The template works on everything from brushing your teeth to preparing a PowerPoint presentation to even lovemaking. What's more, you don't have to learn a different meditation technique for each activity: The Meditation in Action Template can be applied to anything, anytime, and anywhere.

Rather than talking about it, let's try a simple hands-on demonstration of the Meditation in Action Template, using it to do a simple chore that you do every day.

Just One Dish Meditation

To get the feel of the Meditation in Action Template, I'm going to have you wash a single dish. To rephrase the age-old Passover Seder question, "Why is this dish different from all other dishes?" The answer is, it's not, but the *way you wash it* will be.

Do the Just One Dish Meditation when you can be alone. That way you can avoid strange looks from your family, who may wonder why Mommy or Daddy is pretending to be a robot.

JUST ONE DISH MEDITATION INSTRUCTIONS

- Choose a sturdy dish, a sponge, and a drying cloth.

- Plug the sink and set the dish down in it.

- Slowly turn on the water. Listen to the sounds the water makes. Do this just like you did in Naked Sound Meditation.

- Test the water temperature, and make the necessary adjustment so the water is comfortably warm and not too hot.

• Lift the soap dispenser over the sink and slowly squeeze it. Watch as the soap falls and dissolves into the water.

• Watch the water level rise until the sink is half full. Place your hand on the faucet handle and shut off the water. Feel the cool metal in your palm. Notice the momentary cessation of sound.

• Slowly, immerse your hands into the water. Locate the dish and grasp it in one hand. Note how it feels. Slowly lift the dish out of the water and look at it. There may be a coating of shiny suds on the bottom rim. Notice how the dish catches the light. *Really look at this dish.*

• With your other hand, pick up the sponge. Slowly press the sponge against the surface of the dish. Notice how it feels "squishy" in your hand. Press the sponge gently against the dish surface, and notice the pressure.

• Slowly begin to wash the dish. Feel the movement in your wrist as it makes a circular motion. Remember that you are just washing this one dish. There are no other dishes to wash next. *This is the only dish in the entire world!*

• Thoughts such as *This is so stupid!* or *I might as well throw in all the other dishes* may arise. When they do, simply apply what you've learned in your sitting meditation practice: Allow the thoughts. Catch and release them. Watch them rise and fade away. Then, return to washing the dish.

• Look—*really look* at your dish. Notice its texture. Does it reflect light like a diaphanous seashell? Is it dull? Is it like a subtle mirror, reflecting a hazy image of you?

• Slowly rub your sponge over the dish until it is clean. Turn over the dish, and continue. Stay connected to the movement of your hands, the feel of the water, the tickle of the soap bubbles, and the soft pliability of the sponge in your hand.

• When the dish is immaculate, slowly raise it out of the water. Notice how the water beads and forms tiny rivulets as it drips off. Hear the subtle trickle of water as it drizzles into the sink.

• Slowly, pick up your drying towel. Bring the same attention you brought to washing your dish to drying it. Feel the movements. Hear the sounds. Notice the play of light and shadow.

• When you are finished, slowly set down your clean dish.

So how was it? People describe their experience of Just One Dish as eye-opening, sensual, and even exhilarating. If the Meditation in Action Template can transform the ordinary experience of washing a dish into something out of the ordinary, think what it can do for the rest of your life!

LIVING MEDITATION IN ACTION

Incorporating the Meditation in Action Template into your life can transform your experience of it. Here are a few examples of how you can do it:

- **Walking.** The natural act of walking is a great opportunity for Meditation in Action. Go outside and take a mindful, unhurried walk around the block. Or practice Meditation in Action when you walk from your parking space to your office entrance. Notice how walking really feels. Remember, you don't have to move like a stilted robot. Just walk at a slower pace.

- **At the supermarket.** Make this Meditation in Action with a shopping cart. As you slowly glide your cart down the aisle, notice the feel of the handle and hear the squeak as the wheels scoot over the linoleum floor. If you stop at the bakery section, smell the faint aroma of baking pies. Lift a loaf of bread. Feel the firmness of the crust, with just the faintest "give."

- **Exercising.** Instead of mindlessly daydreaming on your StairMaster, treadmill, or exercise bicycle, apply your Meditation in Action Template. Really notice your movement; feel the heat as it builds in your body and the trickle of sweat on your brow.

- **Yoga.** Stay conscious of your yoga postures. Notice when you lose awareness in the transitions between them. Observe with utmost attention the subtle mind and body changes that might arise with even the slightest adjustment to your pose.

An excellent audiotape on meditation and exercise is Shinzen Young's *Meditation in the Zone* (see the resource section for how to get it).

• **Preparing dinner.** Bring the same mindfulness of Just One Dish Meditation to preparing your meal. Choose one dish and prepare it with the utmost attention. Let's say it's a salad. Don't just dump the veggies into the salad bowl. Arrange them slowly, feeling their different textures, the smooth-skinned tomato, and the pebbly skin of the cucumber. Peel an onion with single-minded attention, noticing how it brings a tear to your eye. Really smell the marvelous aroma as you grate your Parmesan cheese.

• **Eating.** We know how elsewhere and elsewhen we can be when we eat: preoccupied with the newspaper, chatting on the phone, watching TV, or jotting down notes for the next meeting. What a perfect time to use the Meditation in Action Template.

First, turn off your radio, TV, and telephone. Now, look at your food. Take a long, slow breath. Really pay attention to what you are about to eat. Does it look inviting? (If not, perhaps you shouldn't eat it.) Lean forward and smell the aroma. Does it bring up thoughts and memories, pulling you out of the present moment?

Feel the weight of the fork in your hand as you place food onto it. Slowly lift a small forkful of food to your mouth.

As it enters your mouth, close your eyes and bring your awareness to the sensation of taste. Are there one or many tastes here? Does one prominent taste subside, replaced by another?

Chew slowly. Set your fork or drinking glass down after each bite or sip. Don't be in a hurry.

• _____. You've got the picture now. Choose your own activity and apply the Meditation in Action Template to it. Remember, you can do this with *anything*!

Remember, Meditation in Action doesn't require that you move in slow motion, as if swimming in maple syrup. By all means, do things at the pace at which they need to be done. It doesn't make sense to do something mindfully yet in a manner that might attract unwanted attention. Then you'd be too busy feeling self-conscious to be mindful.

Use the Meditation in Action Template as often as possible. In fact, start right now! What do you have to do next? Wash the car? Attend a meeting? Coach the soccer team? Register to vote? Great! Do it with the Meditation in Action Template. You will more fully enjoy what you do—because you will more fully do it.

LOVINGKINDNESS: GOING FURTHER

Back in Week Seven, I promised you an expanded lovingkindness section. And see, I didn't forget!

If Lovingkindness Meditation is something that resonates for you, by all means include it in your daily meditation practice. It's quite simple. Here are some suggestions for practicing awareness meditation and Lovingkindness Meditation together in a single period:

• Do Lovingkindness Meditation last.

• Pause for a minute or two between meditation techniques.

• Make sure you're comfortable when you do lovingkindness. Switch to a different position if need be.

• Allow yourself to truly *feel* your lovingkindness phrases. Lovingkindness Meditation is not an intellectual exercise. When you repeat a phrase, drop down from your mind—and into your heart.

• You don't need to time Lovingkindness Meditation periods. Just relax and let it take as long as it takes.

EXTENDING LOVINGKINDNESS PRACTICE TO OTHERS

Like charity, lovingkindness begins at home. Once you begin to develop your capacity for sending yourself best wishes, there's a natural inclination to "forward them on" to the rest of the world.

The following is a classic Lovingkindness Meditation technique that will enable you to do just that:

Choose four different individuals to whom you will send lovingkindness (note: all persons should be currently living):

• Yourself

• A mentor. Someone who *you personally know* and who has had a major positive impact on your life. This could be anyone— from your rabbi to your car mechanic.

• A close personal friend.

• Someone you hardly know. This could be anyone from a new acquaintance to a complete stranger you saw at the bookstore this afternoon.

• A difficult person. Okay, let's be honest—that *gigantic* pain in the neck in your life! Somebody who is driving you crazy, making your life miserable. Family members, bosses, and landlords are always popular choices. If for some reason your life is so serene you can't come up with one—don't worry—you can!

These four people (including you) will be the recipients of your Lovingkindness Meditation. You will, in turn, direct lovingkindness toward each of them, using the same set of phrases.

Remember, the phrases are meant to emanate not from your head, but your heart. Just relax, and let them resonate from that tender yet courageous place.

INSTRUCTIONS
LOVINGKINDNESS MEDITATION

• First, send lovingkindness to yourself:

> May I be free from danger.
> May I be healthy.
> May I be happy.
> May I have ease of being.

• Next, visualize that mentor, the person who has positively influenced your life, and say:

> May you be free from danger.
> May you be healthy.
> May you be happy.
> May you have ease of being.

• Next, visualize your close friend, and do the same thing:

> May you be free from danger.
> May you be healthy.
> May you be happy.
> May you have ease of being.

• Now, send lovingkindness to the stranger. Picture him or her and repeat:

> May you be free from danger.
> May you be healthy.
> May you be happy.
> May you have ease of being.

• Now, send lovingkindness to your difficult person. Picture him or her and say:

> May you be free from danger.
> May you be healthy.
> May you be happy.
> May you have ease of being.

• Finally, send lovingkindness to all beings, everywhere:

> May all beings be free from danger.
> May all beings be healthy.
> May all beings be happy.
> May all beings have ease of being.

The above instructions may appear complicated, leading you to wonder *How in the world am I supposed to remember all this stuff?* But trust me, Lovingkindness Meditation is much simpler to do than to describe.

Essentially, what you're doing is repeating the same phrases and directing them to different people. If, for some reason, you forget the sequence or the phrases or get lost or frustrated— stop! Take a deep breath and relax. Send yourself some lovingkindness. Then, when you're ready, begin again.

You'll be amazed at how quickly you'll get the hang of Lovingkindness Meditation. Like all meditation, lovingkindness "tastes good. And it's good for you, too."

Above all, remember that the *numero uno* thing here is to be kind to *yourself*. Like I've said, lovingkindness, like charity, begins at home.

Q&A: LOVINGKINDNESS

Q: Can I Change the People I Send Lovingkindness To?

If your question is whether you can send lovingkindness to different people, the answer is definitely yes. Just don't do it during the same Lovingkindness Meditation period.

If, on the other hand, your question is about whether sending lovingkindness to someone will cause them to change, I can only say that it is up to that person. Still, extraordinary things can happen when you send lovingkindness to another: You may see them in an entirely different light, whether they change or not. And then the answer to your question would be yes.

As a personal example of this, I once designated my mom as the difficult (okay, very difficult) person in my Lovingkindness Meditation. After several weeks of sending her lovingkindness, one day I found that I had made her my mentor!

From that day forward, I saw my mother in a much more loving way. I started to treat her differently, and our relationship changed for the better. And you know what else? My mom changed. Like I said, lovingkindness can be a powerful practice.

Q: What About That Person I Don't Like or Am Angry At? Why Should I Send Him/Her Lovingkindness?

This may be the most frequently asked question about lovingkindness practice. After all, why in the world should you wish happiness to someone whose only job on the planet, it seems, is to make your life a living hell! ? The answer, surprisingly, is more about you than that miserable so-and-so.

Consider this: How do you feel when you're angry with someone and refuse to forgive them for whatever slight or wrong they've done you? Not terrific, right? Emotions such as resentment, anger, and animosity invariably lead to uncomfortable, stressful, and painful thoughts and feelings.

What this means is that whenever you, the "grudger," find yourself angry at your "grudgee," you're going to pay a price in suffering. And believe it or not, the price to you is much higher than the one you will mete out to them.

Why? Because you are going to feel hurt not once, but *twice!* Once by the person who hurt you, and once by yourself. Ironic, isn't it? Even if you're in the right (which we *always* are!), you're still guaranteed to get the worst end of the deal!

A much better way to do things, in my opinion, is to practice what I call "enlightened selfishness." This means that you make the alleviation of *your own suffering* job number one. First, send lovingkindness to yourself. Then send it to your difficult person. Do this *not for their sake, but for yours*.

And be open to change. One day, you just might find that you are sending lovingkindness to that difficult person, but this time not for your own sake, but theirs. That's why you should always treat your difficult person as a gift: They are helping you draw closer to your true heart.

Q: Can I Create My Own Lovingkindness Phrases?

The phrases used in Lovingkindness Meditation come from your heart, not your head. What matters more than what you say is the *intent* with which you say it.

Nevertheless, I don't advise you to change the phrases given here, at least for the first two months that you practice lovingkindness.

The lovingkindness phrases used in *8 Minute Meditation* are tried and true: They have been employed for thousands of years by hundreds of thousands of people. There's no reason to go shopping for different ones, at least right now.

After you practice lovingkindness for two months and feel comfortable in your practice, you can experiment with different phrases. If you choose to do so, here are some suggestions:

• Do not use more than four lovingkindness phrases at one time. Otherwise, you may be too busy remembering the phrases to properly direct them to those you are sending them to. Most people report that three or four phrases work best. Keep it at that.

• Once you have created a new phrase sequence, stay with it until it has become automatic. Use it for a month. There is no "perfect" lovingkindness phrase that you will find through constant tweaking.

• Use phrases that are clear and simple to remember and say. Avoid double negatives and multi-syllable and confusing words.

• Avoid using lovingkindness as a protection device for specific ailments or medical procedures. A phrase like "May I be free from root canal pain" is not in the spirit of this practice. This is another reason why I recommend that you stay with the basic phrases as given here.

• Don't wish for things. You know, like a Range Rover or that job with the corner office. Lovingkindness Meditation is not a wishing well. Actually, it's much, much better. Wishing wells dry up, but lovingkindness doesn't.

• Use "May I . . ." to introduce a phrase. Some people think it's better to say "I am . . ." instead of "May I. . . ." Lovingkindness Meditation is *not* Positive Affirmation Land, where you visualize yourself getting something. Lovingkindness is about sending your best wishes and thoughts to yourself and others, so that you and they *may,* if that is the way life chooses to unfold, experience safety, health, and peace. Which I hope you always will.

RESOURCES:
MY PERSONAL A-LIST

THIS MORNING, I typed the word *meditation* in the Amazon search window and got a list of 9,934 books. When I did the same on Google, I got 4,760,000 hits!

Your initial reaction to this might (and I hope will) be "Boy, am I glad I found *8 Minute Meditation*." While it's great to have choices, at a certain point the law of diminishing returns kicks in. The fact that there are almost ten thousand meditation books on Amazon could very well be the main reason you were put off by meditation in the first place!

So, with countless books, tapes, and websites to choose from, how do you go about finding ones that can help you? Well, first of all, the good news is that you happened upon *8 Minute Meditation*. If you've gotten something out of the past 8 weeks, you'll probably trust my recommendations as to other materials I think you'll also benefit from. And please know that everything I recommend is *simpatico* with the *8 Minute Meditation* philosophy: No religious agendas. No inscrutable jargon. No spiritual kidding.

You may not realize it, but this is an important moment in your meditation practice. You're open to deepening it, and I want to steer you in that direction.

I make it my business to keep as up to date as possible with new book releases and developments in meditation. Over the past fifteen years, I've read lots of meditation books and visited many websites. I'm very picky when it comes to things I recommend.

In addition to books and tapes, this section also contains resources and suggestions for two other important adjuncts to deepening your meditation practice: meditation retreats and meditation sitting groups.

What follows is my A-list of meditation materials, the one I give to friends, which I consider us to be at this point. Don't be surprised at the brevity of the list. It may be lean, but believe me, it's choice.

By the way, nothing I say should deter you in the least from personal exploration of all the other books, magazines, tapes, teachers, and retreat centers out there. In fact, I encourage it. Remember, the final authority for what works for you is *you*. If you discover something you think is great that you want to share, contact me at the 8minutes.org website. I'll review it, and if it is appropriate, post it for everyone's benefit.

Books

The Light of Discovery, *Toni Packer* (Tuttle Publishing) Although only 123 pages in length, Toni Packer's book abounds in wisdom for meditators at any stage of practice. Toni heads the Springwater Center in Rochester, New York. This book is a compilation of her talks and answers to questions from students as published in the Springwater Center newsletters.

Toni's teachings are down to earth and penetrating. They include discussions of thinking mind, awareness, and many of the subjects I have addressed in the Q&A sections of *8 Minute Meditation*. This little book can be of great value in helping you deepen your practice.

Zen Mind, Beginner's Mind, *Shunryu Suzuki* (Weatherhill) A classic that is accessible to even the beginning meditator.

Shunryu Suzuki was a Zen master who was instrumental in bringing Zen to America. He is respected and revered by all members of the American meditation community. This timeless collection of his talks begins with the famous sentence, "In the beginner's mind there are many possibilities; in the expert's mind there are few." This clear and profound book expands upon the concepts discussed in *8 Minute Meditation*.

365 Nirvana Here and Now, *Josh Baran* (Element) A great contribution from the man who coined the expression "elsewhere and 'elsewhen.' "

Josh's book is a remarkable compendium of timeless wisdom that spans cultures, continents, and traditions from ancient Zen sages to contemporary poets—all celebrating the perfection of the present moment. These stories, dialogues, songs, and poetry can lend great support in your daily meditation practice; they're like one-a-day vitamins for your mind. *365 Nirvana Here and Now* also contains Josh's own dialogues on presence. Whether you're Oprah or not, this is a great book to have on your nightstand.

Wide Awake, *Diana Winston* (Perigee) Although the subtitle of Diana's book is *A Buddhist Guide for Teens,* this book is perfect for anyone of any age and any religious (or nonreligious) persuasion. As Diana says, "many people, whether or not they are Buddhists, find the insights of Buddhism so helpful that they simply apply them to their lives." *Wide Awake* is a joyful, clear-eyed, and practical guide to integrating meditation into "The Big Picture."

Faith: Trusting Your Own Deepest Experience, *Sharon Salzberg* (Penguin) Not only is Sharon one of our country's foremost meditation teachers, she has authored some important books.

Faith is one of the most honest books ever written as well as one of the most insightful. If you have ever questioned what "faith" means and wondered about your own, Sharon's book will provide you with answers, comfort, and assurance. Her book will also give you immense gratitude for being fortunate enough to have a meditation practice.

The Best Guide to Meditation, *Victor Davich* (St. Martin's Press) Before the Dummies and the Idiots books, there was *The Best Guide to Meditation,* written by yours truly. Its 300+ pages are chock-full of everything you always wanted to know about meditation.

If you're interested in things like sixty-four additional meditation techniques or meditation's connection with Buddhism and other religious traditions, my book might be your cup of green tea. There are also in-depth chapters on Meditation in Action, sitting postures, and an entire section devoted to the application of meditation in pain management.

Audio and Video Tapes

One of the great advances in the teaching and practice of meditation over the past decade has been in the area of audiotapes. While there is no substitute for personal interaction with a great meditation teacher (which I always recommend), audio and video tapes provide us with the next best thing—and with far greater convenience.

There's a special experience in actually hearing a good teacher speak his or her own words; it transmits something beyond words. In my opinion, the more you listen to a good meditation teacher, the more likely that something good will "rub off" on you.

It used to be that if you wanted to study with a good meditation teacher, you had to go to where they were holding a retreat. This could sometimes mean a trek clear across the country, and considerable time and expense. Today, with just the click of your mouse, you can access hundreds of talks, guided meditations, and other teaching materials from some of the foremost meditation teachers in the country. I highly recommend that you take advantage of their audio and video tapes.

Here are three places I direct friends to when they ask about meditation tapes and videos. These websites are extremely well organized and complete. If you have questions, call them.

Sounds True, www.soundstrue.com, 800-333-9185
Sounds True offers more than five hundred titles that run the

gamut of spiritual subjects, including psychology, health and healing, self-discovery, and, of course, meditation. The Sounds True meditation collection also features several meditation books on tape. You can sample many of these materials on the Internet before ordering them. Recommended titles: *Meditations of the Heart,* Jack Kornfield; *When Things Fall Apart,* Pema Chodron; *Natural Meditation* (video), Surya Das; *Road Sage,* Sylvia Boorstein; *Radical Self-Acceptance,* Tara Brach.

Dharma Seed Tape Library, www.dharmaseed.org, 800-969-7333 Dharma Seed Tape Library publishes a variety of live recordings from nationally known western meditation teachers, including IMS founders Sharon Salzberg and Joseph Goldstein. These are mostly recorded talks and not studio produced materials. Nevertheless, you'll find the overall audio quality very good. All materials are reasonably priced, and some are available on a donation basis.

Dharma Seed (and Sounds True) offer my number-one top choice in the audiotape area: *Insight Meditation: A Complete Correspondence Course,* by Sharon Salzberg and Joseph Goldstein. If you have any thoughts of taking your meditation practice to the next level, I highly recommend it.

Other titles: *Approaches to Meditation,* Christina Feldman; *Wise Effort and the Practices of Awakening,* Tara Brach; *Metta: Loving Yourself,* Sharon Salzberg; *Four Foundations of Mindfulness* (video), Carol Wilson; *Vipassana Video Retreat.*

The Dharma Seed website also offers **Dharmastream, www.dharmastream.org**. Here you can sample, for free, more than thirty recorded meditation talks from meditation teachers who teach at the Spirit Rock Retreat Center and IMS Meditation

Center (see below). This is a great way to get an idea of what to order and also be introduced to teachers who you may someday want to join on a retreat.

Shinzen Young Website, www.shinzen.org Shinzen Young is an American who trained extensively in Asian monasteries. He has, for the past thirty years, taught and led retreats across America and Canada.

I've already mentioned that Shinzen was my primary meditation teacher. I am delighted to be able to offer you a way that you, too, can receive the benefits of his cogent, accessible, and modern teaching methods.

Shinzen's taped talks and guided meditations are topical, down to earth, and transformative. His website contains a classified catalog of more than one hundred taped talks and guided meditations. They include tapes on Vipassana Meditation (similar to what you've been doing these past 8 weeks), Christian and Jewish meditation, and the science-meditation interface.

Recommended titles: *The Formula; Beginner's Guide to Meditation; Millennium Album III—Guided Meditations; Break Through Difficult Emotions; Carrying Meditation into Life; Meditation in the Zone; Shinzen's 20-minute Relaxation.*

Meditation Retreat Centers

Permanent meditation retreat centers in America are scarce. But the good news is that two wonderful permanent retreat centers exist, located on both the east and west coasts: IMS, in Barre, Massachusetts, and Spirit Rock, in Marin County, California.

These not-for-profit retreat centers teach in the Vipassana, or Insight Meditation tradition, which is what informs the meditation techniques you have learned in *8 Minute Meditation*. IMS and Spirit Rock are impeccably managed and maintained by a community of meditators and teachers. Prices to attend retreats vary, but every attempt is made to keep them affordable. Scholarships are also available. Teachers' fees for leading retreats are usually separate from room and board and made on a donation basis, which in the Buddhist teaching tradition is called *dana*.

If you aspire to become a serious meditator, a retreat at IMS or Spirit Rock is one of the greatest gifts you can give yourself.

The Insight Meditation Society (IMS), Barre, MA, www.dharma.org, 978-355-4378 IMS was founded in 1975 as a nonprofit organization to provide an environment conducive to the practice of Insight and Lovingkindness Meditation. The center is set on 160 secluded acres in Barre, Massachusetts, whose town motto is "Tranquil and Alert."

IMS offers a full year-round schedule of silent meditation retreats lasting in duration from one weekend to three months. Recent special retreats include those for women, young adults, and people of color.

A group of senior teachers provides regular and ongoing guidance and direction and teaches a number of courses each year. They include Sharon Salzberg, Joseph Goldstein, Lama Surya Das, and Christina Feldman.

Spirit Rock Meditation Center, Fairfax, CA, www.spiritrock.org, 415-488-0164 Like IMS, Spirit Rock Meditation

Center is dedicated to the practice of mindful awareness through Vipassana Meditation.

The Spirit Rock property, located in Marin County, California, covers more than four hundred acres and is secluded and breathtaking. The center hosts a full program of ongoing classes, one-day retreats, and longer residential retreats. Recent offerings include "Vipassana 101" and "One Breath at a Time: Buddhism and the Twelve Steps."

The meditation halls and accommodations at Spirit Rock are immaculate, classic, and state-of-the art. My personal experience as a retreatant here was quite wonderful.

Several well-known meditation teachers and book authors lead retreats at Spirit Rock. They include Spirit Rock founder Jack Kornfield, Sylvia Boorstein, and Anna Douglas.

Vipassana Support International (VSI), www.shinzen.org, 866-666-0874 VSI is a nonprofit, nondenominational organization dedicated to those who desire to deepen their meditation practice through the practice of Vipassana Meditation. VSI coordinates Shinzen Young's national retreat schedule throughout the United States and Canada. The VSI website contains information on upcoming retreats, events, and other information.

VSI does not have a permanent retreat center site. Instead, Shinzen Young travels widely around the country to different facilities where the VSI retreats are held. If you go to his website, you may find that Shinzen may soon be "appearing at a retreat near you."

There are other retreat centers and retreats located throughout the country. You might find out about them by asking around your local meditation community. Also, meditation and yoga magazines such as *Tricycle* and *Yoga Journal* usually contain advertisements and listings for retreats and retreat centers. There's also the Internet, where you'll even find a website completely devoted to retreat centers: www.retreatfinder.com.

Meditation Sitting Groups

The practice of meditation in America is growing and spreading rapidly across the continent as well as around the world. In a recent survey, over ten million Americans said that they meditate. One indication of this growth is the proliferation of meditation sitting groups. At these gatherings, usually held once a week, meditators convene to meditate, support, and help each other.

Sitting groups provide something of great value: a standing date with meditation that you look forward to keeping. I have regularly attended a weekly meditation group at my friend Ann's house for more than ten years, and it has reinforced my own daily meditation practice enormously.

Sitting groups also provide you the opportunity to meet and meditate with other like-minded people in your community—who also seem to bring the most delicious baked goods! When you're ready to find your meditation sitting group, here are some suggestions:

• Consult your local merchants and bulletin boards. Next time you're at your yoga class, health food store, coffee hangout, or spiritual bookshop, ask around among the workers and shoppers as to the whereabouts of a meditation sitting group. Check the bulletin boards as well. Do the same at your local college campus, health club, and, believe it or not, the Y.

• Obtain a copy of *Inquiring Mind,* the journal of the national meditation community. Besides being a great magazine, it contains listings of upcoming retreats and established sitting groups throughout America. The *Mind* is published quarterly on a contribution basis. You'll find them on the web at www.inquiringmind.com.

If for some reason you cannot find a sitting group in your area, start one of your own. It's easy and not a big deal. All you need is at least one fellow meditator, a timer, and a bag of chocolate-chip cookies (which will make other meditators show up in no time flat!).

Meditation sitting groups are informal, free-form affairs, so make up your own agenda. You might decide that you'll meditate for a certain amount of time. And if anyone needs to stop sooner, that's fine. You might also, at some point, play a teaching tape or do a guided meditation, with one person as the "narrator." The sitting group I belong to sits in a circle after meditation and discusses how meditation practice supported and helped our lives over the previous week.

Whether you join an ongoing sitting group or start your own, you'll be doing something positive to nourish and deepen your meditation practice. You'll also be helping other like-minded people. It's win-win, all the way.

The Official 8 Minute Meditation Website, www.8minutes.org

Now here's a website I can personally recommend—mine! I created 8minutes.org to support your continuation with what I hope has become, and will be, your daily, lifetime meditation practice.

Here is where you will find the latest and the greatest 8 Minute Meditation developments. It's also the place where you can order the *8 Minute Guided Meditation* CD, which allows you to close your eyes and follow the weekly meditation instructions presented in *8 Minute Meditation*.

Other features you'll find at www.8minutes.org include:

- **More Q&As.** Just because you've completed the 8 Minute Meditation program doesn't mean you have to stop asking questions. As you deepen your practice, expect more to come up. Send them in to me, and I'll answer them for you and everybody.

- **Links to new developments, retreat centers, and resources.** Like I said, at last count, more than 10 million Americans said they meditate. Every week, more articles appear about meditation and its benefits. The website will keep you up to date on the latest developments in meditation, including scientific studies, retreat centers, and noteworthy books, tapes, and videos—all of which will carry the *8 Minute Meditation* Seal of Approval.

IN CLOSING

WELL, I GUESS that's all I have to say—for now. Except for something I've already said to you 8 times before, modified just a tad. And that is . . .

You're doing great! Just turn the page and move on with your life—with meditation at your side.

May this book benefit you, and everyone you come in contact with.

May you be happy.

—Victor

THANK YOU ⏱

BOY, HOW DO those Oscar winners do it? Sixty seconds to thank everyone. I don't know where to start. But that hasn't stopped me yet.

First, I express deepest gratitude to mentor and close friend Josh Baran. Josh has been instrumental in the creation, writing, and publicizing of *8 Minute Meditation,* from proposal to making sure I was interviewed by *Time* magazine. Josh's benevolence also extends to letting me occupy the famous "Baran author couch" in his loft on my trips to New York.

Tremendous thanks go out to the folks at my agency, Lowenstein-Yost. To Eileen Cope, that rare agent who tells you she's going to sell your book—and by gosh does it. Eileen "XO" to *you*! Also to business affairs maven Norman Kurz, who let me play lawyer—and then provided the reality check. As did Marty Weisberg, Esq., valued friend and counselor.

Over at Perigee Books, this year's Nobel Peace Prize goes to my amazing editor, Christel Winkler: guide, guardian, confidant, and all-around smart cookie. Her equanimity level approaches the Dalai Lama's—and she needed it at times to handle yours truly.

Thanks also to Perigee publisher John Duff, who had the foresight to acquire *8 Minute Meditation* and give it his full support. My deep respect to the designers, salespeople, publicists, and everyone else at Perigee for their graciousness in inviting me to put my two cents into everything from front cover to text font. I hear you're all recovering nicely.

Great gratitude to my longtime meditation teacher, coach, and friend, Shinzen Young, not only for his conveyance of the teachings, but for helping me get my first book deal. I've known Shinzen for twenty years and his unflagging energy and compassion are awe inspiring.

Deep thanks to teachers and friends Sharon Salzberg and Catherine Ingram, who provide a sanctuary of truth, beauty, caring, and humor to all.

Re lovingkindness, I send *mucho* to dear friend Ann Buck, whose loyalty, generosity, encouragement, and support have sustained me through it all. Ann is a living embodiment of the true spirit of compassion.

Many other teachers have influenced my development as a meditator and author through my contact with them or exposure to their books and teachings. Among those I thank are Shunryu Suzuki Roshi, Taizan Maezumi Roshi, the Dalai Lama, Bernie Glassman, Wolfgang Kopp, Thomas Merton, Ajhan Chah, Alan Watts,

Steve Hagen, Jack Kornfield, Toni Packer, Pema Chodron, Joan Tol-lifson, Christina Feldman, Joseph Goldstein, and Sylvia Boorstein.

Heartfelt acknowledgment to close chum, Reverend John Newton, for his unswerving faith in my ability to write this book, no matter what I said. John read several drafts and his advice to "stop already!" was golden. Speaking of manuscript review, no one does it better than Reed Moran, my longtime buddy, confi-dant, cheerleader—and the best writer in Hollywood.

Thanks go out to my unofficial marketing advisors: Helen Boehm, Susan Anderson, Cathy Moran, my niece Arlyn Davich, and Mike Attie. Also to Steve Royes, who tested the program and provided feedback.

Thanks to Joe Besch, elder statesman at Barnes and Noble, for reminding me to believe, and to Stan and the staff at the Bodhi Tree Bookstore—for not charging me rent. And a big Downward Facing Dog to everyone at Sacred Movement Yoga in Venice, es-pecially my teachers Brad, Julie, Jason, Ira, and Lynda.

Finally, eternal love and gratitude to Dr. D, true-blue brother Mitchell, who always sings to me on my birthday.

I think they're signaling me from the control booth. Yup, time's up. Just as well. As they say, "After the ecstasy, the laundry." And boy, has it piled up.

ABOUT THE AUTHOR

Victor Davich has been a meditator for over twenty years. He has studied with some of America's foremost meditation teachers. His first book, *The Best Guide to Meditation,* is highly popular and published in four languages.

In the business world, Victor has worked both as a copywriter and attorney for major advertising agencies and motion picture studios, including McCann-Erickson, Young & Rubicam, and Paramount Pictures. He has also written many movie-marketing campaigns, co-produced the feature film *The Brain,* created the NBC primetime series *Nasty Boys,* and authored five screenplays.

Victor lives at the beach in Southern California, where, in great gratitude, he walks and meditates daily.

ABOUT THE AUTHOR

Victor Davich has been a meditator for over twenty years. He has studied with some of America's foremost meditation teachers. His first book, *The Best Guide to Meditation,* is highly popular and published in four languages.

In the business world, Victor has worked both as a copywriter and attorney for major advertising agencies and motion picture studios, including McCann-Erickson, Young & Rubicam, and Paramount Pictures. He has also written many movie-marketing campaigns, co-produced the feature film *The Brain,* created the NBC primetime series *Nasty Boys,* and authored five screenplays.

Victor lives at the beach in Southern California, where, in great gratitude, he walks and meditates daily.